55 Appetizer Recipes for Home

By: Kelly Johnson

Table of Contents

Appetizers:

- Spinach and Artichoke Dip
- Caprese Skewers with Balsamic Glaze
- Bacon-Wrapped Jalapeño Poppers
- Deviled Eggs with Smoked Salmon
- Bruschetta with Tomato and Basil
- Shrimp Cocktail
- Stuffed Mushrooms with Cream Cheese and Herbs
- Mozzarella Sticks with Marinara Sauce
- Cucumber Bites with Feta and Dill
- Guacamole with Homemade Tortilla Chips
- Chicken Satay with Peanut Sauce
- Mini Quiches with Spinach and Feta
- Buffalo Chicken Dip
- Asian Spring Rolls with Shrimp and Peanut Dipping Sauce
- Baked Brie with Raspberry Jam and Almonds
- Prosciutto-Wrapped Asparagus Spears
- Sweet Potato Fritters with Garlic Aioli
- Mini Chicken Tacos with Lime Crema
- Smoked Salmon Canapés
- Cajun Spiced Popcorn Shrimp
- Stuffed Bell Peppers with Creamy Cheese
- Teriyaki Chicken Skewers
- Crab Cakes with Remoulade Sauce
- Greek Salad Skewers
- Bacon-Wrapped Dates with Goat Cheese
- Chicken Wings with Honey Sriracha Glaze
- Crostini with Roasted Red Pepper Hummus
- Sausage Stuffed Jalapeños
- Spicy Tuna Tartare on Wonton Crisps
- Caramelized Onion and Gruyere Tartlets
- Coconut Shrimp with Mango Dipping Sauce
- Tomato Basil Bruschetta
- Pigs in a Blanket with Dijon Mustard
- Avocado Egg Rolls with Sweet Chili Sauce
- Parmesan and Herb-Stuffed Cherry Tomatoes

- BBuffalo Cauliflower Bites
- Cheese and Herb-Stuffed Puff Pastry Twists
- Crispy Zucchini Fries with Garlic Aioli
- Lobster and Avocado Wonton Cups
- Smoky Chipotle Meatballs
- Edamame and Ginger Potstickers
- Sesame Ginger Chicken Lettuce Wraps
- Roasted Red Pepper and Walnut Dip (Muhammara)
- Spicy Mango Salsa with Tortilla Chips
- Crispy Polenta Bites with Gorgonzola
- Chorizo-Stuffed Mushrooms
- Sun-Dried Tomato and Basil Pinwheels
- Cucumber Cups with Crab Salad
- Pesto and Sun-Dried Tomato Cheese Ball
- Mango Habanero Glazed Meatballs
- Feta and Spinach Stuffed Phyllo Cups
- Cajun Shrimp and Grits Bites
- Brussels Sprouts Sliders with Bacon and Balsamic Glaze
- Curry Chicken Salad on Cucumber Rounds
- Blue Cheese and Walnut-Stuffed Grapes

Spinach and Artichoke Dip

Ingredients:

- 1 (10-ounce) package frozen chopped spinach, thawed and drained
- 1 (14-ounce) can artichoke hearts, drained and chopped
- 1/2 cup mayonnaise
- 1/2 cup sour cream
- 1 cup grated Parmesan cheese
- 1 cup shredded mozzarella cheese
- 1 teaspoon minced garlic
- 1/2 teaspoon salt
- 1/4 teaspoon black pepper
- 1/4 teaspoon red pepper flakes (optional)
- Tortilla chips, crackers, or sliced baguette for serving

Instructions:

Preheat your oven to 375°F (190°C).
In a medium-sized bowl, combine the chopped spinach, chopped artichoke hearts, mayonnaise, sour cream, Parmesan cheese, mozzarella cheese, minced garlic, salt, black pepper, and red pepper flakes (if using). Mix everything together until well combined.
Transfer the mixture to a baking dish, spreading it out evenly.
Bake in the preheated oven for about 25-30 minutes or until the dip is hot and bubbly, and the top is golden brown.
Remove from the oven and let it cool slightly before serving.
Serve the Spinach and Artichoke Dip with tortilla chips, crackers, or sliced baguette.

Feel free to customize the recipe to your liking. Some variations include adding cream cheese for extra creaminess, using different types of cheese, or incorporating additional herbs and spices.

This delicious dip is sure to be a hit at your next party or gathering!

Caprese Skewers with Balsamic Glaze

Ingredients:

- Cherry tomatoes
- Fresh mozzarella balls (bocconcini)
- Fresh basil leaves
- Balsamic glaze
- Extra-virgin olive oil
- Salt and pepper, to taste
- Wooden skewers

Instructions:

Prepare Skewers:
- Soak wooden skewers in water for at least 30 minutes to prevent them from burning during cooking.
- Assemble the skewers by threading one cherry tomato, one mozzarella ball, and one fresh basil leaf onto each skewer.

Arrange Skewers:
- Place the assembled skewers on a serving platter.

Drizzle with Balsamic Glaze:
- In a small bowl, mix balsamic glaze with a touch of extra-virgin olive oil. Drizzle the mixture over the skewers.

Season:
- Sprinkle salt and pepper over the skewers to taste.

Serve:
- Arrange the skewers on a serving platter and serve immediately.

Optional Garnish:
- Optionally, garnish with additional fresh basil leaves and a light drizzle of balsamic glaze for a decorative touch.

Variations:
- Try adding a sprinkle of dried oregano or a dash of garlic powder for additional flavor.
- For a festive touch, use colored toothpicks or skewers.

Tips:
- Use the freshest ingredients for the best flavor. Look for ripe cherry tomatoes, fresh basil, and high-quality mozzarella.

- If you don't have balsamic glaze, you can reduce balsamic vinegar in a saucepan over low heat until it thickens.

Enjoy these Caprese Skewers with Balsamic Glaze as a delightful and visually appealing appetizer!

Deviled Eggs with Smoked Salmon

Ingredients:

- 6 large eggs
- 2 tablespoons mayonnaise
- 1 teaspoon Dijon mustard
- 1 teaspoon white wine vinegar
- Salt and pepper, to taste
- 2 ounces smoked salmon, finely chopped
- Fresh dill, for garnish
- Paprika, for garnish

Instructions:

Hard Boil the Eggs:
- Place the eggs in a single layer in a saucepan and cover with water. Bring the water to a boil, then reduce the heat to a simmer and cook the eggs for 10-12 minutes. Once cooked, transfer the eggs to an ice bath to cool.

Peel and Halve Eggs:
- Peel the cooled eggs and cut them in half lengthwise. Remove the yolks and place them in a bowl.

Prepare Filling:
- Mash the egg yolks with a fork. Add mayonnaise, Dijon mustard, white wine vinegar, salt, and pepper. Mix until well combined.

Add Smoked Salmon:
- Fold in the finely chopped smoked salmon into the yolk mixture. Ensure it's evenly distributed.

Fill the Egg Whites:
- Spoon or pipe the smoked salmon and yolk mixture into the egg white halves.

Garnish:
- Garnish each deviled egg with a small piece of smoked salmon, a sprinkle of paprika, and a small sprig of fresh dill.

Chill:
- Refrigerate the deviled eggs for at least 30 minutes to allow the flavors to meld.

Serve:
- Arrange the deviled eggs on a serving platter and serve chilled.

Optional Variations:
- Add a touch of horseradish for extra kick.
- Garnish with capers or chives for added flavor.

Enjoy these Deviled Eggs with Smoked Salmon as an elegant and tasty appetizer for any occasion!

Bruschetta with Tomato and Basil

Ingredients:

- Baguette or Italian bread, sliced
- 4-5 ripe tomatoes, diced
- 1/4 cup fresh basil leaves, finely chopped
- 2 cloves garlic, minced
- 3 tablespoons extra-virgin olive oil
- 1 tablespoon balsamic vinegar
- Salt and pepper, to taste
- Optional: Balsamic glaze for drizzling

Instructions:

Preheat Oven:
- Preheat the oven to 375°F (190°C).

Toast the Bread:
- Arrange the sliced baguette or Italian bread on a baking sheet. Toast in the preheated oven for 5-7 minutes or until golden brown. Alternatively, you can grill the bread for a smoky flavor.

Prepare Tomato Basil Mixture:
- In a bowl, combine diced tomatoes, chopped basil, minced garlic, extra-virgin olive oil, balsamic vinegar, salt, and pepper. Mix well to ensure the flavors meld.

Let it Marinate:
- Allow the tomato basil mixture to marinate for at least 15-20 minutes to let the flavors infuse.

Assemble Bruschetta:
- Spoon the tomato basil mixture generously onto each toasted bread slice.

Optional Drizzle:
- For an extra burst of flavor, drizzle a bit of balsamic glaze over each bruschetta.

Serve:
- Arrange the bruschetta on a serving platter and serve immediately.

Variations:
- Add mozzarella slices on top of the tomato mixture before serving for a Caprese twist.
- Sprinkle feta cheese or Parmesan on top for added richness.

Tips:
- Use fresh and ripe tomatoes for the best flavor.
- Rub the toasted bread with a clove of garlic for an additional layer of garlic flavor.

Enjoy this classic Bruschetta with Tomato and Basil as a refreshing and vibrant appetizer!

Shrimp Cocktail

Ingredients:

For the Shrimp:

- 1 pound large shrimp, peeled and deveined
- 1 tablespoon olive oil
- 1 teaspoon Old Bay seasoning (optional)
- Salt and pepper, to taste

For the Cocktail Sauce:

- 1 cup ketchup
- 2 tablespoons prepared horseradish
- 1 tablespoon lemon juice
- 1 teaspoon Worcestershire sauce
- Hot sauce, to taste (optional)
- Salt and pepper, to taste

For Garnish:

- Fresh lemon wedges
- Fresh parsley, chopped

Instructions:

Cook the Shrimp:
- In a large pot, bring water to a boil. Season with salt and add the shrimp. Cook for 3-4 minutes or until the shrimp turn pink and opaque. Drain and immediately transfer to an ice bath to stop the cooking process.

Season the Shrimp:
- In a bowl, toss the cooked and cooled shrimp with olive oil, Old Bay seasoning (if using), salt, and pepper. Chill in the refrigerator.

Prepare Cocktail Sauce:
- In another bowl, mix together ketchup, horseradish, lemon juice, Worcestershire sauce, hot sauce (if using), salt, and pepper. Adjust the ingredients to your taste preferences.

Chill Sauce:

- Refrigerate the cocktail sauce for at least 30 minutes to allow the flavors to meld.

Serve:
- Arrange the chilled shrimp on a serving platter with a bowl of the cocktail sauce in the center.

Garnish:
- Garnish with fresh lemon wedges and chopped parsley.

Optional Presentation:
- For an elegant presentation, serve the shrimp cocktail in individual glasses or on a bed of ice.

Variations:
- Add a splash of vodka to the cocktail sauce for a Shrimp Cocktail Martini.
- Include finely diced cucumber, avocado, or red onion for extra freshness.

Tips:
- Choose high-quality, fresh shrimp for the best taste.
- Adjust the spiciness of the cocktail sauce according to your preference.

Enjoy this classic Shrimp Cocktail as a refreshing and delightful appetizer!

Stuffed Mushrooms with Cream Cheese and Herbs

Ingredients:

- 20-24 large mushrooms, cleaned and stems removed
- 8 oz (225g) cream cheese, softened
- 1/4 cup grated Parmesan cheese
- 2 cloves garlic, minced
- 1 tablespoon fresh parsley, finely chopped
- 1 teaspoon fresh thyme leaves, chopped
- Salt and pepper, to taste
- Olive oil for drizzling
- Breadcrumbs (optional, for topping)

Instructions:

Preheat the Oven:
- Preheat your oven to 375°F (190°C).

Prepare Mushrooms:
- Clean the mushrooms with a damp cloth and remove the stems. Set aside.

Make Filling:
- In a bowl, combine softened cream cheese, grated Parmesan, minced garlic, chopped parsley, chopped thyme, salt, and pepper. Mix until well combined.

Stuff the Mushrooms:
- Using a small spoon, fill each mushroom cap with the cream cheese mixture, pressing it down gently.

Drizzle with Olive Oil:
- Place the stuffed mushrooms on a baking sheet. Drizzle each stuffed mushroom with a bit of olive oil.

Optional Breadcrumbs:
- If desired, sprinkle breadcrumbs over the stuffed mushrooms for a crispy topping.

Bake:
- Bake in the preheated oven for 15-20 minutes or until the mushrooms are tender and the filling is golden.

Garnish:
- Remove from the oven and let them cool slightly. Garnish with additional chopped parsley if desired.

Serve:
- Arrange the stuffed mushrooms on a serving platter and serve warm.

Variations:
- Add cooked and crumbled bacon to the cream cheese mixture for a smoky flavor.
- Mix in finely chopped spinach or sun-dried tomatoes for additional depth.

Tips:
- Choose mushrooms with a good size and shape for stuffing.
- Make sure the cream cheese is at room temperature to make mixing easier.

These Stuffed Mushrooms with Cream Cheese and Herbs make a delightful appetizer for any gathering or party. Enjoy!

Mozzarella Sticks with Marinara Sauce

Ingredients:

For Mozzarella Sticks:

- 1 pound (about 16 sticks) mozzarella cheese, cut into sticks
- 1 cup all-purpose flour
- 3 large eggs, beaten
- 2 cups breadcrumbs (seasoned or plain)
- 1 teaspoon garlic powder
- 1 teaspoon dried oregano
- Salt and pepper, to taste
- Cooking oil, for frying

For Marinara Sauce:

- 1 can (14 ounces) crushed tomatoes
- 2 cloves garlic, minced
- 1 teaspoon dried basil
- 1 teaspoon dried oregano
- 1/2 teaspoon onion powder
- Salt and pepper, to taste
- 1 tablespoon olive oil
- Optional: Red pepper flakes for heat

Instructions:

Prepare Mozzarella Sticks:
- In three separate bowls, place the flour in one, beaten eggs in another, and combine breadcrumbs with garlic powder, dried oregano, salt, and pepper in the third.

Coat Mozzarella Sticks:
- Dip each mozzarella stick into the flour, then into the beaten eggs, and finally into the breadcrumb mixture, ensuring they are evenly coated. Repeat the process for a thicker coating if desired.

Freeze:

- Place the coated mozzarella sticks on a baking sheet lined with parchment paper and freeze for at least 30 minutes. This helps set the coating and prevents the cheese from melting too quickly during frying.

Make Marinara Sauce:
- In a saucepan, heat olive oil over medium heat. Add minced garlic and sauté until fragrant. Add crushed tomatoes, dried basil, dried oregano, onion powder, salt, pepper, and optional red pepper flakes. Simmer for 15-20 minutes, stirring occasionally.

Fry Mozzarella Sticks:
- Heat cooking oil in a deep fryer or a heavy-bottomed pan to 350°F (180°C). Fry the mozzarella sticks in batches for 2-3 minutes or until golden brown. Remove with a slotted spoon and place on a paper towel-lined plate to drain excess oil.

Serve:
- Arrange the mozzarella sticks on a serving platter with a side of warm marinara sauce for dipping.

Garnish:
- Optionally, garnish with fresh chopped parsley or grated Parmesan.

Enjoy:
- Serve the mozzarella sticks with marinara sauce while they are still hot and gooey.

Note: Be cautious when frying to avoid oil splatter.

These Mozzarella Sticks with Marinara Sauce make for a delicious and crowd-pleasing appetizer. Enjoy!

Cucumber Bites with Feta and Dill

Ingredients:

- 2 large English cucumbers, sliced into rounds
- 1 cup crumbled feta cheese
- 1/4 cup fresh dill, finely chopped
- 1/4 cup cherry tomatoes, diced (optional, for garnish)
- 2 tablespoons extra-virgin olive oil
- 1 tablespoon red wine vinegar
- Salt and pepper, to taste

Instructions:

Prepare Cucumbers:
- Wash the cucumbers thoroughly. Cut them into thick rounds, about 1/2 inch thick.

Make Feta and Dill Mixture:
- In a bowl, combine crumbled feta and finely chopped fresh dill. Mix well.

Assemble Cucumber Bites:
- Place a small spoonful of the feta and dill mixture on each cucumber round.

Add Tomato Garnish (Optional):
- If using, top each cucumber bite with a small amount of diced cherry tomatoes for a burst of color and flavor.

Drizzle with Olive Oil and Vinegar:
- In a separate small bowl, whisk together extra-virgin olive oil and red wine vinegar. Drizzle this mixture over the cucumber bites.

Season:
- Sprinkle salt and pepper over the cucumber bites to taste.

Serve:
- Arrange the cucumber bites on a serving platter and serve immediately.

Garnish (Optional):
- Optionally, garnish with additional fresh dill for a decorative touch.

Variations:
- Add a small dollop of tzatziki sauce on top for extra creaminess.
- Sprinkle with a pinch of black sesame seeds for an elegant touch.

Tips:
- Choose firm cucumbers with a smooth skin for the best texture.

- Adjust the amount of feta, dill, and other ingredients according to your taste preferences.

These Cucumber Bites with Feta and Dill make a refreshing and light appetizer, perfect for any gathering or summer event. Enjoy!

Guacamole with Homemade Tortilla Chips

Ingredients:

For Guacamole:

- 3 ripe avocados
- 1 small red onion, finely diced
- 2 tomatoes, diced
- 1-2 cloves garlic, minced
- 1 jalapeño, seeds removed and finely chopped
- 1/4 cup fresh cilantro, chopped
- Juice of 2 limes
- Salt and pepper, to taste

For Homemade Tortilla Chips:

- 8-10 small corn tortillas
- Olive oil
- Salt, to taste

Instructions:

Guacamole:

    Prepare Avocados:
- Cut the avocados in half, remove the pit, and scoop the flesh into a mixing bowl.

    Mash Avocados:
- Mash the avocados with a fork or potato masher, leaving some chunks for texture.

    Add Vegetables:
- Add diced red onion, tomatoes, minced garlic, chopped jalapeño, and chopped cilantro to the mashed avocados.

    Add Lime Juice:
- Squeeze the juice of two limes over the mixture.

    Season:
- Season the guacamole with salt and pepper to taste. Mix everything together until well combined.

    Cover and Chill:

- Cover the guacamole with plastic wrap, ensuring it directly touches the surface to prevent browning. Refrigerate until ready to serve.

Homemade Tortilla Chips:

Preheat Oven:
- Preheat your oven to 350°F (175°C).

Cut Tortillas:
- Stack the corn tortillas and cut them into triangles.

Arrange on Baking Sheet:
- Arrange the tortilla triangles in a single layer on baking sheets.

Brush with Olive Oil:
- Lightly brush both sides of each triangle with olive oil.

Season with Salt:
- Sprinkle salt over the oiled tortilla triangles.

Bake:
- Bake in the preheated oven for 10-12 minutes or until the tortillas are golden brown and crispy. Keep an eye on them to prevent burning.

Cool:
- Allow the homemade tortilla chips to cool completely.

Serve:
- Serve the guacamole with the homemade tortilla chips on the side for dipping.

Optional:
- Garnish the guacamole with additional cilantro or a slice of lime before serving.

Tips:

- Adjust the spiciness of the guacamole by adding more or less jalapeño.
- For extra flavor, consider adding a pinch of cumin or a dash of hot sauce to the guacamole.
- Serve the homemade tortilla chips warm for the best taste and texture.

This Guacamole with Homemade Tortilla Chips is a classic and delicious snack, perfect for parties or gatherings. Enjoy!

Chicken Satay with Peanut Sauce

Ingredients:

For Chicken Satay:

- 1.5 pounds boneless, skinless chicken breasts or thighs, cut into thin strips
- 1/4 cup soy sauce
- 2 tablespoons honey
- 2 tablespoons curry powder
- 2 cloves garlic, minced
- 1 tablespoon ginger, grated
- Wooden skewers, soaked in water for 30 minutes

For Peanut Sauce:

- 1 cup creamy peanut butter
- 1/4 cup soy sauce
- 2 tablespoons rice vinegar
- 2 tablespoons honey
- 1 tablespoon sesame oil
- 1 teaspoon ginger, grated
- 1 clove garlic, minced
- 1/2 cup coconut milk
- 1 tablespoon lime juice
- Red pepper flakes (optional, for heat)
- Chopped peanuts and fresh cilantro for garnish

Instructions:

Chicken Satay:

> Marinate Chicken:
> - In a bowl, mix together soy sauce, honey, curry powder, minced garlic, and grated ginger. Add the chicken strips and marinate for at least 30 minutes, or preferably, overnight in the refrigerator.
>
> Thread Chicken on Skewers:
> - Thread the marinated chicken strips onto the soaked wooden skewers.
>
> Grill or Broil:

- Grill the chicken skewers on a preheated grill or broil in the oven for about 5-7 minutes per side or until fully cooked and slightly charred.

Peanut Sauce:
- In a saucepan over medium heat, combine peanut butter, soy sauce, rice vinegar, honey, sesame oil, grated ginger, minced garlic, coconut milk, and lime juice. Stir continuously until well combined and heated through.
- Optional: Add red pepper flakes for a spicy kick.

Serve:
- Arrange the grilled chicken satay on a serving platter.

Garnish:
- Drizzle peanut sauce over the chicken satay and garnish with chopped peanuts and fresh cilantro.

Serve with Extra Sauce:
- Serve additional peanut sauce on the side for dipping.

Tips:

- Adjust the level of sweetness or spiciness in the peanut sauce according to your preference.
- For added flavor, you can sprinkle chopped cilantro and a squeeze of lime juice over the grilled chicken just before serving.
- If using wooden skewers, remember to soak them in water for at least 30 minutes before threading the chicken to prevent them from burning during cooking.

This Chicken Satay with Peanut Sauce is a flavorful and crowd-pleasing appetizer or main dish. Enjoy!

Mini Quiches with Spinach and Feta

Ingredients:

For the Mini Quiches:

- 1 package (about 12 ounces) refrigerated pie crusts or homemade pie crust
- 1 cup fresh spinach, chopped
- 1/2 cup feta cheese, crumbled
- 1/4 cup grated Parmesan cheese
- 3 large eggs
- 1 cup milk or half-and-half
- 1/2 teaspoon salt
- 1/4 teaspoon black pepper
- 1/4 teaspoon ground nutmeg (optional)
- Cooking spray or melted butter for greasing

Instructions:

Preheat Oven:
- Preheat your oven to 375°F (190°C).

Prepare Pie Crusts:
- If using refrigerated pie crusts, roll out the crusts and cut circles to fit into the mini muffin tin. Press the crusts into each cup, making sure they go up the sides. If using homemade pie crust, roll out the dough and cut circles.

Precook Pie Crusts (Optional):
- Optionally, you can pre-bake the crusts for about 5 minutes to prevent sogginess. Prick the bottoms with a fork before baking.

Prepare Filling:
- In a bowl, whisk together eggs, milk or half-and-half, salt, pepper, and nutmeg if using.

Add Spinach and Cheese:
- Add chopped spinach, feta cheese, and grated Parmesan to the egg mixture. Mix until well combined.

Fill Mini Muffin Cups:
- Spoon the spinach and feta mixture into each mini muffin cup over the pie crust.

Bake:

- Bake in the preheated oven for 15-18 minutes or until the mini quiches are set and the edges are golden brown.

Cool:
- Allow the mini quiches to cool in the muffin tin for a few minutes, then transfer them to a wire rack to cool completely.

Serve:
- Serve the mini quiches warm or at room temperature.

Tips:

- Customize the fillings by adding sautéed mushrooms, diced tomatoes, or caramelized onions.
- Ensure that the spinach is well-drained to prevent excess moisture in the quiches.
- These mini quiches can be made ahead and reheated in the oven or microwave before serving.

Enjoy these Mini Quiches with Spinach and Feta as a delightful and bite-sized appetizer!

Buffalo Chicken Dip

Ingredients:

- 2 cups shredded cooked chicken (rotisserie or cooked and shredded boneless, skinless chicken breasts)
- 1 package (8 ounces) cream cheese, softened
- 1/2 cup buffalo sauce (adjust to taste for spice level)
- 1/2 cup ranch dressing
- 1 cup shredded cheddar cheese
- 1/2 cup crumbled blue cheese
- 1/4 cup green onions, chopped (optional, for garnish)
- Tortilla chips, celery sticks, or sliced baguette for serving

Instructions:

Preheat Oven:
- Preheat your oven to 375°F (190°C).

Prepare Baking Dish:
- Grease a baking dish or oven-safe skillet.

Mix Ingredients:
- In a large mixing bowl, combine shredded chicken, softened cream cheese, buffalo sauce, ranch dressing, shredded cheddar cheese, and crumbled blue cheese. Mix until all ingredients are well combined.

Transfer to Baking Dish:
- Transfer the mixture to the prepared baking dish, spreading it evenly.

Bake:
- Bake in the preheated oven for 20-25 minutes or until the dip is hot and bubbly, and the top is golden brown.

Garnish:
- If desired, garnish the Buffalo Chicken Dip with chopped green onions.

Serve:
- Serve the dip hot, straight from the oven, with tortilla chips, celery sticks, or sliced baguette for dipping.

Tips:

- Adjust the amount of buffalo sauce to your preferred spice level.
- Feel free to add more cheese on top for an extra cheesy finish.

- You can make this dip ahead of time and refrigerate it, then bake it just before serving.

Variations:

- Mix in a layer of blue cheese or cheddar cheese on top before baking for an extra cheesy crust.
- Add diced celery or red pepper for added crunch and flavor.

Enjoy this Buffalo Chicken Dip as a crowd-pleasing and zesty appetizer for your next gathering or game day!

Asian Spring Rolls with Shrimp and Peanut Dipping Sauce

Ingredients:

For Spring Rolls:

- 8-10 rice paper wrappers
- 1 cup cooked shrimp, peeled, deveined, and chopped
- 1 cup rice vermicelli noodles, cooked and cooled
- 1 cup shredded lettuce
- 1 cup julienned carrots
- 1 cucumber, julienned
- Fresh mint leaves
- Fresh cilantro leaves

For Peanut Dipping Sauce:

- 1/3 cup creamy peanut butter
- 2 tablespoons soy sauce
- 2 tablespoons rice vinegar
- 1 tablespoon honey
- 1 clove garlic, minced
- 1 teaspoon grated ginger
- 2-3 tablespoons water (adjust for desired consistency)

Instructions:

Prepare Ingredients:

Cook Shrimp and Noodles:
- Cook shrimp and rice vermicelli noodles according to package instructions. Allow them to cool before assembling the spring rolls.

Prepare Vegetables:
- Julienne the carrots and cucumber. Shred the lettuce. Arrange mint leaves and cilantro leaves.

Assemble Spring Rolls:

- Fill a shallow dish with warm water. Dip one rice paper wrapper into the water for about 10-15 seconds until it softens but is still slightly firm.
- Lay the softened rice paper on a clean, damp surface. Place a small handful of shredded lettuce, a portion of shrimp, rice vermicelli noodles, julienned carrots, cucumber, mint leaves, and cilantro leaves on the lower half of the rice paper.
- Fold the sides of the rice paper over the filling and then roll it up tightly from the bottom, forming a spring roll. Repeat with the remaining ingredients.

Make Peanut Dipping Sauce:
- In a bowl, whisk together peanut butter, soy sauce, rice vinegar, honey, minced garlic, grated ginger, and water. Adjust the consistency with more water if needed.

Serve:
- Serve the Asian Spring Rolls with the Peanut Dipping Sauce on the side.

Tips:

- Work with one rice paper wrapper at a time to prevent them from sticking together.
- Customize the filling with your favorite vegetables or add cooked chicken or tofu for variation.
- Serve the spring rolls immediately or cover them with a damp cloth to prevent them from drying out.

These Asian Spring Rolls with Shrimp and Peanut Dipping Sauce make for a fresh, flavorful, and healthy appetizer or light meal. Enjoy!

Baked Brie with Raspberry Jam and Almonds

Ingredients:

- 1 wheel of Brie cheese (about 8 ounces)
- 1/2 cup raspberry jam
- 1/4 cup sliced almonds
- 1 tablespoon honey
- Crackers, baguette slices, or apple slices for serving

Instructions:

Preheat Oven:
- Preheat your oven to 350°F (175°C).

Prepare Brie:
- Place the Brie wheel on a baking sheet lined with parchment paper.

Score the Top:
- Using a sharp knife, gently score the top rind of the Brie in a crosshatch pattern.

Spread Raspberry Jam:
- Spread raspberry jam evenly over the top of the Brie.

Add Almonds:
- Sprinkle sliced almonds over the raspberry jam, covering the surface.

Drizzle with Honey:
- Drizzle honey over the top of the almonds.

Bake:
- Bake in the preheated oven for 12-15 minutes or until the Brie is soft and gooey.

Serve:
- Carefully transfer the baked Brie to a serving platter. Serve it warm with crackers, baguette slices, or apple slices for dipping.

Tips:

- You can adjust the sweetness by using more or less raspberry jam and honey based on your preference.
- Feel free to experiment with different types of jams or preserves for a variety of flavors.

- Serve the baked Brie immediately for the best texture and flavor.

This Baked Brie with Raspberry Jam and Almonds is a delightful appetizer that combines the creaminess of Brie with the sweetness of raspberry and the crunch of almonds. Enjoy!

Prosciutto-Wrapped Asparagus Spears

Ingredients:

- 1 bunch of fresh asparagus spears, woody ends trimmed
- 8-10 slices of prosciutto
- Olive oil for drizzling
- Freshly ground black pepper
- Balsamic glaze (optional, for drizzling)
- Grated Parmesan cheese (optional, for garnish)

Instructions:

Preheat Oven:
- Preheat your oven to 400°F (200°C).

Prepare Asparagus:
- Trim the woody ends from the asparagus spears.

Wrap with Prosciutto:
- Take one slice of prosciutto and wrap it around each asparagus spear, spiraling it along the length. Repeat for all asparagus spears.

Arrange on Baking Sheet:
- Place the prosciutto-wrapped asparagus spears on a baking sheet lined with parchment paper, ensuring they are spaced apart.

Drizzle with Olive Oil:
- Drizzle olive oil over the prosciutto-wrapped asparagus. Use your hands to coat the asparagus evenly.

Season:
- Grind black pepper over the asparagus to taste. Remember that prosciutto is already salty, so you may not need additional salt.

Bake:
- Bake in the preheated oven for about 12-15 minutes or until the asparagus is tender, and the prosciutto is crispy.

Optional Finish:
- If desired, drizzle with balsamic glaze and sprinkle with grated Parmesan cheese just before serving.

Serve:
- Arrange the prosciutto-wrapped asparagus spears on a serving platter and serve immediately.

Tips:

- Choose asparagus spears that are uniform in size for even cooking.
- Make sure to trim the woody ends of the asparagus to ensure a tender result.
- If you don't have balsamic glaze, you can reduce balsamic vinegar in a saucepan until it thickens.

These Prosciutto-Wrapped Asparagus Spears make for an elegant and delicious appetizer or side dish. Enjoy!

Sweet Potato Fritters with Garlic Aioli

Ingredients:

For Sweet Potato Fritters:

- 2 medium sweet potatoes, peeled and grated
- 1 small onion, finely diced
- 1/2 cup all-purpose flour
- 2 large eggs, beaten
- 1 teaspoon baking powder
- 1 teaspoon smoked paprika
- Salt and pepper, to taste
- Vegetable oil for frying

For Garlic Aioli:

- 1/2 cup mayonnaise
- 1 clove garlic, minced
- 1 tablespoon fresh lemon juice
- Salt and pepper, to taste
- Fresh parsley, chopped (optional, for garnish)

Instructions:

Sweet Potato Fritters:

   Prepare Sweet Potatoes:
   - Peel and grate the sweet potatoes. Place them in a clean kitchen towel and squeeze out any excess moisture.

   Mix Ingredients:
   - In a large bowl, combine grated sweet potatoes, diced onion, all-purpose flour, beaten eggs, baking powder, smoked paprika, salt, and pepper. Mix until well combined.

   Heat Oil:
   - Heat vegetable oil in a skillet over medium-high heat.

   Fry Fritters:
   - Drop spoonfuls of the sweet potato mixture into the hot oil, pressing them down slightly to form fritters. Fry until golden brown on both sides, about 3-4 minutes per side. Cook in batches to avoid overcrowding the skillet.

Drain Excess Oil:
- Place the cooked fritters on a plate lined with paper towels to drain any excess oil.

Garlic Aioli:

Prepare Aioli:
- In a small bowl, mix mayonnaise, minced garlic, fresh lemon juice, salt, and pepper. Adjust the seasonings to your taste.

Serve:
- Serve the sweet potato fritters hot with a side of garlic aioli.

Garnish (Optional):
- Garnish with chopped fresh parsley for a burst of color and freshness.

Tips:

- You can add a pinch of cayenne pepper or red pepper flakes to the sweet potato mixture for a spicy kick.
- Test the oil's temperature by dropping a small amount of the batter into it. It should sizzle and brown within a few seconds.

Enjoy these Sweet Potato Fritters with Garlic Aioli as a tasty and satisfying appetizer or side dish!

Mini Chicken Tacos with Lime Crema

Ingredients:

For Mini Chicken Tacos:

- 1 pound boneless, skinless chicken breasts, cooked and shredded
- 1 packet taco seasoning
- Mini flour or corn tortillas
- 1 cup shredded lettuce
- 1 cup diced tomatoes
- 1 cup shredded cheddar or Mexican blend cheese
- Fresh cilantro, chopped (for garnish)
- Lime wedges (for serving)

For Lime Crema:

- 1/2 cup sour cream
- 1 tablespoon fresh lime juice
- 1 teaspoon lime zest
- Salt and pepper, to taste

Instructions:

Mini Chicken Tacos:

    Cook and Shred Chicken:
- Cook the chicken breasts and shred them using two forks. Toss the shredded chicken with taco seasoning according to package instructions.

    Prepare Toppings:
- Dice tomatoes, shred lettuce, and chop fresh cilantro. Set aside.

    Warm Tortillas:
- Heat mini tortillas in a dry skillet or warm them in the oven according to package instructions.

    Assemble Tacos:
- Spoon a portion of the seasoned shredded chicken onto each mini tortilla.

    Add Toppings:

- Top with shredded lettuce, diced tomatoes, and shredded cheese.

Garnish:
- Garnish with chopped cilantro and serve with lime wedges on the side.

Lime Crema:

Make Lime Crema:
- In a bowl, mix together sour cream, fresh lime juice, lime zest, salt, and pepper. Adjust the seasonings to your taste.

Serve:
- Serve the mini chicken tacos with a drizzle of lime crema.

Tips:

- Customize the toppings with your favorite ingredients like diced avocados, salsa, or sliced jalapeños.
- You can use store-bought or homemade tortillas for the mini tacos.
- Add a dash of hot sauce to the lime crema for a spicy kick.

Enjoy these Mini Chicken Tacos with Lime Crema as a delicious and bite-sized appetizer or party snack!

Smoked Salmon Canapés

Ingredients:

- 1 baguette, thinly sliced
- 8 ounces smoked salmon, sliced
- 1/2 cup cream cheese, softened
- 2 tablespoons fresh dill, chopped
- 1 tablespoon capers, drained
- 1 small red onion, thinly sliced
- Lemon wedges, for serving

Instructions:

Slice Baguette:
- Preheat the oven to 350°F (175°C). Arrange the baguette slices on a baking sheet and toast them in the oven until golden and crisp, about 5-7 minutes.

Prepare Cream Cheese Mixture:
- In a bowl, mix the softened cream cheese with chopped fresh dill.

Assemble Canapés:
- Spread a thin layer of the dill-infused cream cheese on each toasted baguette slice.
- Top each slice with a piece of smoked salmon.
- Garnish with sliced red onion and capers.

Garnish:
- Garnish the smoked salmon canapés with additional fresh dill.

Serve:
- Arrange the canapés on a serving platter and serve with lemon wedges on the side.

Tips:

- Make sure the cream cheese is at room temperature for easy spreading.
- Experiment with different types of bread, such as rye or pumpernickel, for added variety.
- If you'd like a bit of heat, you can add a sprinkle of black pepper or a dash of hot sauce to the cream cheese mixture.

These Smoked Salmon Canapés make for an elegant and flavorful appetizer, perfect for gatherings and special occasions. Enjoy!

Cajun Spiced Popcorn Shrimp

Ingredients:

For Popcorn Shrimp:

- 1 pound small shrimp, peeled and deveined
- 1 cup buttermilk
- 1 cup all-purpose flour
- 1 cup cornmeal
- 2 teaspoons Cajun seasoning
- 1 teaspoon garlic powder
- 1 teaspoon onion powder
- 1/2 teaspoon smoked paprika
- Salt and black pepper, to taste
- Vegetable oil, for frying

For Cajun Dipping Sauce:

- 1/2 cup mayonnaise
- 1 tablespoon Dijon mustard
- 1 tablespoon Cajun seasoning
- 1 tablespoon fresh lemon juice
- 1 teaspoon hot sauce (optional, for extra heat)

Instructions:

Popcorn Shrimp:

  Marinate Shrimp:
  - In a bowl, marinate the peeled and deveined shrimp in buttermilk for at least 30 minutes or up to 2 hours.

  Prepare Coating:
  - In a separate bowl, mix together flour, cornmeal, Cajun seasoning, garlic powder, onion powder, smoked paprika, salt, and black pepper.

  Coat Shrimp:
  - Remove the shrimp from the buttermilk and coat each shrimp in the seasoned flour-cornmeal mixture, pressing the coating gently to adhere.

  Heat Oil:

- Heat vegetable oil in a deep fryer or a heavy-bottomed pan to 350°F (175°C).

Fry Shrimp:
- Fry the popcorn shrimp in batches for 2-3 minutes or until golden brown and crispy. Use a slotted spoon to transfer them to a paper towel-lined plate to drain excess oil.

Cajun Dipping Sauce:

Make Dipping Sauce:
- In a small bowl, whisk together mayonnaise, Dijon mustard, Cajun seasoning, fresh lemon juice, and hot sauce (if using). Adjust the seasonings to your taste.

Serve:
- Serve the Cajun Spiced Popcorn Shrimp hot with the Cajun dipping sauce on the side.

Tips:

- Adjust the level of Cajun seasoning and hot sauce in both the coating and the dipping sauce according to your spice preference.
- Serve the popcorn shrimp with lemon wedges for an extra burst of freshness.

Enjoy these Cajun Spiced Popcorn Shrimp as a flavorful and crispy appetizer or snack!

Stuffed Bell Peppers with Creamy Cheese

Ingredients:

- 4 large bell peppers (any color)
- 1 pound ground beef or turkey
- 1 cup cooked rice
- 1 cup black beans, drained and rinsed
- 1 cup corn kernels (fresh, frozen, or canned)
- 1 cup diced tomatoes
- 1 cup shredded cheddar cheese
- 1 cup shredded Monterey Jack cheese
- 1/2 cup diced onions
- 2 cloves garlic, minced
- 1 teaspoon ground cumin
- 1 teaspoon chili powder
- Salt and pepper, to taste
- 1 cup tomato sauce or salsa
- Fresh cilantro, chopped (for garnish)

Instructions:

Preheat Oven:
- Preheat your oven to 375°F (190°C).

Prepare Bell Peppers:
- Cut the tops off the bell peppers and remove the seeds and membranes. If needed, trim the bottoms slightly to help them stand upright in the baking dish.

Brown Ground Meat:
- In a skillet over medium heat, brown the ground beef or turkey until fully cooked. Drain any excess fat.

Cook Onions and Garlic:
- Add diced onions and minced garlic to the skillet. Sauté until the onions are translucent.

Add Vegetables and Seasonings:
- Stir in cooked rice, black beans, corn, diced tomatoes, ground cumin, chili powder, salt, and pepper. Cook for an additional 3-5 minutes until the mixture is well combined and heated through.

Stir in Cheese:

- Remove the skillet from heat and stir in shredded cheddar and Monterey Jack cheese until melted and incorporated.

Stuff Bell Peppers:
- Stuff each bell pepper with the meat and cheese mixture, pressing down gently.

Arrange in Baking Dish:
- Place the stuffed bell peppers in a baking dish. Pour tomato sauce or salsa over the top.

Bake:
- Cover the baking dish with foil and bake in the preheated oven for 25-30 minutes or until the peppers are tender.

Top with Cheese (Optional):
- Remove the foil, sprinkle additional cheese on top of each stuffed pepper, and bake for an additional 5-7 minutes or until the cheese is melted and bubbly.

Serve:
- Garnish with chopped cilantro and serve the stuffed bell peppers hot.

Tips:

- Feel free to customize the filling by adding ingredients like diced jalapeños, olives, or green onions.
- For a vegetarian version, replace the ground meat with plant-based alternatives or add extra beans and vegetables.

These Stuffed Bell Peppers with Creamy Cheese make for a satisfying and delicious meal. Enjoy!

Teriyaki Chicken Skewers

Ingredients:

For Teriyaki Marinade:

- 1/2 cup soy sauce
- 1/4 cup mirin (Japanese sweet rice wine)
- 2 tablespoons sake (or white wine)
- 2 tablespoons brown sugar
- 1 tablespoon honey
- 2 cloves garlic, minced
- 1 teaspoon fresh ginger, grated
- 1 tablespoon cornstarch (optional, for thickening)

For Chicken Skewers:

- 1.5 pounds boneless, skinless chicken thighs or chicken breasts, cut into bite-sized pieces
- Wooden skewers, soaked in water for at least 30 minutes
- Sesame seeds, for garnish (optional)
- Green onions, sliced, for garnish (optional)

Instructions:

Teriyaki Marinade:

Prepare Marinade:
- In a bowl, whisk together soy sauce, mirin, sake, brown sugar, honey, minced garlic, and grated ginger until well combined. If you prefer a thicker sauce, you can add cornstarch by mixing it with a bit of water and stirring it into the marinade.

Chicken Skewers:

Marinate Chicken:
- Place the chicken pieces in a shallow dish or a resealable plastic bag. Pour half of the teriyaki marinade over the chicken, reserving the other half for basting and serving. Marinate the chicken in the refrigerator for at least 30 minutes or up to 4 hours.

Skewer Chicken:
- Preheat the grill or grill pan to medium-high heat. Thread the marinated chicken pieces onto the soaked wooden skewers.

Grill:
- Grill the chicken skewers for 6-8 minutes per side, basting with the reserved teriyaki marinade during the last few minutes of cooking. Ensure the chicken reaches an internal temperature of 165°F (74°C).

Garnish:
- Remove the skewers from the grill, and garnish with sesame seeds and sliced green onions if desired.

Serve:
- Serve the Teriyaki Chicken Skewers over rice or with your favorite side dishes, and drizzle with additional teriyaki sauce.

Tips:

- If using wooden skewers, remember to soak them in water for at least 30 minutes before threading the chicken to prevent them from burning during grilling.
- Adjust the sweetness or saltiness of the teriyaki marinade to your liking by tweaking the amount of honey or soy sauce.
- You can add extra vegetables like bell peppers, onions, or pineapple chunks to the skewers for added flavor.

Enjoy these Teriyaki Chicken Skewers as a delicious and flavorful dish!

Crab Cakes with Remoulade Sauce

Ingredients:

For Crab Cakes:

- 1 pound lump crab meat, drained
- 1/2 cup mayonnaise
- 1 large egg, beaten
- 1 tablespoon Dijon mustard
- 1 tablespoon Worcestershire sauce
- 1 teaspoon Old Bay seasoning
- 1/2 cup breadcrumbs
- 2 tablespoons fresh parsley, chopped
- Salt and pepper, to taste
- 2 tablespoons unsalted butter (for frying)
- Lemon wedges, for serving

For Remoulade Sauce:

- 1/2 cup mayonnaise
- 2 tablespoons Dijon mustard
- 1 tablespoon capers, chopped
- 1 tablespoon pickle relish
- 1 tablespoon fresh parsley, chopped
- 1 teaspoon hot sauce (adjust to taste)
- 1 teaspoon Worcestershire sauce
- Salt and pepper, to taste

Instructions:

Crab Cakes:

Prepare Crab Mixture:
- In a large bowl, gently fold together lump crab meat, mayonnaise, beaten egg, Dijon mustard, Worcestershire sauce, Old Bay seasoning, breadcrumbs, and chopped parsley. Season with salt and pepper to taste.

Form Crab Cakes:
- Shape the crab mixture into patties, about 1/2 to 3/4 inch thick. Place them on a baking sheet lined with parchment paper.

Chill:
- Refrigerate the crab cakes for at least 30 minutes to help them firm up.

Cook Crab Cakes:
- In a skillet over medium heat, melt butter. Fry the crab cakes for 4-5 minutes per side or until golden brown and cooked through.

Remoulade Sauce:

Make Remoulade Sauce:
- In a bowl, whisk together mayonnaise, Dijon mustard, capers, pickle relish, chopped parsley, hot sauce, Worcestershire sauce, salt, and pepper. Adjust the seasonings to your taste.

Serve:
- Serve the Crab Cakes hot with a dollop of Remoulade Sauce on top. Garnish with additional chopped parsley and lemon wedges.

Tips:

- Be gentle when mixing the crab cake ingredients to preserve the lump crab meat's texture.
- If you prefer, you can bake the crab cakes in a preheated oven at 375°F (190°C) for about 15-20 minutes until they are cooked through.
- Adjust the spiciness of the Remoulade Sauce by adding more or less hot sauce.

Enjoy these Crab Cakes with Remoulade Sauce as a delightful appetizer or main dish!

Greek Salad Skewers

Ingredients:

For Salad Skewers:

- Cherry tomatoes
- Cucumber, cut into chunks
- Kalamata olives, pitted
- Feta cheese, cubed
- Red onion, cut into wedges

For Greek Salad Dressing:

- 1/4 cup extra-virgin olive oil
- 2 tablespoons red wine vinegar
- 1 teaspoon dried oregano
- 1 teaspoon honey or maple syrup
- Salt and black pepper, to taste

Instructions:

Greek Salad Dressing:

Prepare Dressing:
- In a small bowl, whisk together olive oil, red wine vinegar, dried oregano, honey or maple syrup, salt, and black pepper. Set aside.

Greek Salad Skewers:

Assemble Skewers:
- Thread cherry tomatoes, cucumber chunks, Kalamata olives, feta cheese cubes, and red onion wedges onto skewers in a colorful and appealing order.

Drizzle with Dressing:
- Place the assembled skewers on a serving platter and drizzle the Greek Salad Dressing over the top.

Serve:
- Serve the Greek Salad Skewers immediately as a refreshing appetizer or side dish.

Tips:

- You can customize the skewers by adding ingredients like marinated artichoke hearts, pepperoncini, or grilled chicken.
- If using wooden skewers, soak them in water for about 30 minutes before threading to prevent them from burning.

These Greek Salad Skewers offer a convenient and delightful way to enjoy the flavors of a classic Greek salad in a fun and portable format. Enjoy!

Bacon-Wrapped Dates with Goat Cheese

Ingredients:

- Medjool dates, pitted
- Goat cheese, softened
- Bacon slices, cut in half
- Toothpicks

Instructions:

Preheat Oven:
- Preheat your oven to 375°F (190°C).

Prepare Dates:
- Make a small slit in each pitted date, creating an opening for stuffing.

Stuff with Goat Cheese:
- Fill each date with a small amount of softened goat cheese. You can use a spoon or a piping bag to make this process easier.

Wrap with Bacon:
- Take a half-slice of bacon and wrap it around each stuffed date, securing it with a toothpick.

Arrange on Baking Sheet:
- Place the bacon-wrapped dates on a baking sheet lined with parchment paper, with the loose end of the bacon facing down.

Bake:
- Bake in the preheated oven for 15-20 minutes or until the bacon is crispy and browned.

Broil (Optional):
- If the bacon needs additional crisping, you can broil the bacon-wrapped dates for a couple of minutes, keeping a close eye to prevent burning.

Serve:
- Remove the toothpicks, arrange the bacon-wrapped dates on a serving platter, and serve them warm.

Tips:

- Experiment with different types of goat cheese, such as herbed or honey-infused, for added flavor.

- You can drizzle honey over the bacon-wrapped dates before serving for a sweet touch.

These Bacon-Wrapped Dates with Goat Cheese make for a delightful and savory appetizer, combining sweet, savory, and creamy flavors. Enjoy!

Chicken Wings with Honey Sriracha Glaze

Ingredients:

For Chicken Wings:

- 2 pounds chicken wings, split at joints, tips discarded
- 1 tablespoon vegetable oil
- Salt and black pepper, to taste
- 1 teaspoon garlic powder
- 1 teaspoon onion powder
- 1 teaspoon paprika
- 1 teaspoon baking powder (optional, for extra crispiness)

For Honey Sriracha Glaze:

- 1/3 cup honey
- 1/4 cup Sriracha sauce (adjust to taste)
- 2 tablespoons soy sauce
- 1 tablespoon rice vinegar
- 1 teaspoon sesame oil (optional)
- 1 tablespoon fresh cilantro, chopped (for garnish)
- Sesame seeds (for garnish)

Instructions:

Chicken Wings:

    Preheat Oven:
- Preheat your oven to 400°F (200°C).

    Prepare Wings:
- In a large bowl, toss the chicken wings with vegetable oil, salt, black pepper, garlic powder, onion powder, and paprika. If desired, add baking powder to enhance crispiness.

    Bake:
- Place the wings on a baking sheet lined with parchment paper, making sure they are not touching. Bake in the preheated oven for 45-50 minutes or until the wings are golden and crispy.

Honey Sriracha Glaze:

Make Glaze:
- In a saucepan over medium heat, combine honey, Sriracha sauce, soy sauce, rice vinegar, and sesame oil. Stir well and let it simmer for 3-5 minutes, allowing the flavors to meld. Adjust the Sriracha sauce to your desired level of spiciness.

Coat Wings:
- Once the wings are cooked, transfer them to a large bowl. Pour the Honey Sriracha Glaze over the wings and toss until they are evenly coated.

Garnish:
- Garnish the wings with chopped cilantro and sesame seeds.

Serve:
- Serve the Chicken Wings with Honey Sriracha Glaze hot, and enjoy them with your favorite dipping sauce on the side.

Tips:

- For extra crispiness, you can broil the wings for an additional 2-3 minutes after coating them with the glaze.
- Adjust the honey and Sriracha ratios to balance sweetness and spiciness according to your taste preferences.
- Serve with ranch or blue cheese dressing and celery sticks for a classic pairing.

These Chicken Wings with Honey Sriracha Glaze are perfect for a flavorful and slightly spicy appetizer or game-day snack. Enjoy!

Crostini with Roasted Red Pepper Hummus

Ingredients:

For Roasted Red Pepper Hummus:

- 1 can (15 ounces) chickpeas, drained and rinsed
- 1/2 cup roasted red peppers (from a jar), drained
- 1/4 cup tahini
- 2 tablespoons lemon juice
- 2 cloves garlic, minced
- 1/2 teaspoon ground cumin
- Salt and pepper, to taste
- 2-3 tablespoons extra-virgin olive oil (plus extra for drizzling)

For Crostini:

- Baguette, thinly sliced
- Olive oil for brushing
- Fresh parsley, chopped (for garnish)

Instructions:

Roasted Red Pepper Hummus:

Prepare Chickpeas:
- In a food processor, combine chickpeas, roasted red peppers, tahini, lemon juice, minced garlic, cumin, salt, and pepper.

Blend:
- Blend the ingredients until smooth. While blending, drizzle in the olive oil gradually until the hummus reaches your desired consistency.

Adjust Seasoning:
- Taste the hummus and adjust the seasoning, adding more salt, pepper, or lemon juice if needed.

Crostini:

Preheat Oven:
- Preheat your oven to 375°F (190°C).

Slice Baguette:
- Slice the baguette into thin rounds. Place the slices on a baking sheet.

Brush with Olive Oil:
- Brush each slice of baguette lightly with olive oil.

Bake:
- Bake in the preheated oven for 8-10 minutes or until the crostini are golden and crispy.

Serve:
- Once the crostini are done, let them cool slightly. Spread a generous amount of Roasted Red Pepper Hummus on each crostini.

Garnish:
- Garnish with chopped fresh parsley and drizzle with a little extra olive oil.

Tips:

- Experiment with additional toppings like crumbled feta cheese, chopped olives, or a sprinkle of paprika.
- If you don't have roasted red peppers from a jar, you can roast fresh red peppers in the oven and peel them before adding to the hummus.
- Customize the crostini by rubbing them with a garlic clove before brushing with olive oil for an extra layer of flavor.

These Crostini with Roasted Red Pepper Hummus make for a tasty and elegant appetizer for any occasion. Enjoy!

Sausage Stuffed Jalapeños

Ingredients:

- 12-15 fresh jalapeños
- 1/2 pound ground sausage (pork or turkey)
- 4 ounces cream cheese, softened
- 1 cup shredded cheddar cheese
- 1 teaspoon garlic powder
- 1 teaspoon onion powder
- Salt and black pepper, to taste
- 1/2 cup breadcrumbs (optional, for topping)
- Fresh cilantro or parsley, chopped (for garnish)

Instructions:

Preheat Oven:
- Preheat your oven to 375°F (190°C).

Prepare Jalapeños:
- Cut the jalapeños in half lengthwise and remove the seeds and membranes. Use caution and wear gloves to protect your hands from the heat.

Cook Sausage:
- In a skillet over medium heat, cook the ground sausage until browned and cooked through. Drain any excess fat.

Make Filling:
- In a bowl, combine the cooked sausage, softened cream cheese, shredded cheddar cheese, garlic powder, onion powder, salt, and black pepper. Mix until well combined.

Stuff Jalapeños:
- Spoon the sausage and cheese mixture into each jalapeño half, pressing it in firmly.

Optional Breadcrumb Topping:
- If desired, sprinkle breadcrumbs over the top of the stuffed jalapeños for added texture.

Bake:
- Place the stuffed jalapeños on a baking sheet lined with parchment paper. Bake in the preheated oven for 15-20 minutes or until the jalapeños are tender and the filling is bubbly.

Broil (Optional):
- If you like a crispy top, you can broil the stuffed jalapeños for an additional 2-3 minutes until the breadcrumbs are golden brown.

Garnish:
- Garnish with chopped cilantro or parsley.

Serve:
- Serve the Sausage Stuffed Jalapeños warm as an appetizer or party snack.

Tips:

- You can customize the level of spiciness by choosing jalapeños with more or fewer seeds.
- Experiment with different cheeses or add diced bacon for extra flavor.
- Adjust the filling ingredients to your taste preferences, adding more spices or herbs as desired.

These Sausage Stuffed Jalapeños are a flavorful and spicy appetizer that's perfect for parties or gatherings. Enjoy responsibly!

Spicy Tuna Tartare on Wonton Crisps

Ingredients:

For Tuna Tartare:

- 1/2 pound sushi-grade tuna, finely diced
- 2 tablespoons soy sauce
- 1 tablespoon sesame oil
- 1 tablespoon sriracha sauce (adjust to taste)
- 1 teaspoon fresh ginger, minced
- 1 teaspoon sesame seeds
- 1 green onion, thinly sliced
- 1 teaspoon lime juice
- Salt and black pepper, to taste

For Wonton Crisps:

- Wonton wrappers, cut into squares or triangles
- Vegetable oil for frying

For Garnish:

- Avocado, diced
- Cucumber, diced
- Fresh cilantro or microgreens

Instructions:

Tuna Tartare:

   Prepare Tuna:
   - In a bowl, combine finely diced tuna, soy sauce, sesame oil, sriracha sauce, minced ginger, sesame seeds, sliced green onion, lime juice, salt, and black pepper. Mix gently to combine. Adjust seasoning to taste.

Wonton Crisps:

   Cut Wonton Wrappers:
   - Cut wonton wrappers into squares or triangles.

Fry Wonton Crisps:
- Heat vegetable oil in a pan or deep fryer to 350°F (175°C). Fry the wonton wrappers in batches until they are golden brown and crispy. Remove with a slotted spoon and place them on a paper towel-lined plate to drain excess oil.

Assembly:

Serve on Wonton Crisps:
- Spoon a small amount of spicy tuna tartare onto each wonton crisp.

Add Garnishes:
- Top the tuna with diced avocado, cucumber, and a sprinkle of fresh cilantro or microgreens.

Serve:
- Arrange the Spicy Tuna Tartare on Wonton Crisps on a serving platter and serve immediately.

Tips:

- Use a sharp knife to finely dice the tuna for a smooth and delicate texture.
- Adjust the level of spiciness by adding more or less sriracha sauce.
- Customize the garnishes with your favorite ingredients, such as radishes, jalapeños, or tobiko (fish roe).

These Spicy Tuna Tartare on Wonton Crisps make for an elegant and flavorful appetizer, perfect for entertaining or special occasions. Enjoy!

Caramelized Onion and Gruyere Tartlets

Ingredients:

For Tartlet Shells:

- 1 package (about 14 ounces) pre-made puff pastry, thawed
- Flour for dusting

For Caramelized Onions:

- 2 large onions, thinly sliced
- 2 tablespoons unsalted butter
- 1 tablespoon olive oil
- 1 teaspoon sugar
- Salt and black pepper, to taste
- 2 tablespoons balsamic vinegar (optional)

For Filling:

- 1 cup Gruyere cheese, shredded
- Fresh thyme leaves, for garnish

Instructions:

Tartlet Shells:

    Preheat Oven:
- Preheat your oven to 400°F (200°C).

    Roll Out Puff Pastry:
- On a lightly floured surface, roll out the puff pastry to about 1/8 inch thickness.

    Cut Tartlet Rounds:
- Using a round cookie cutter or a glass, cut out rounds of puff pastry and press them into a mini muffin tin.

    Bake:
- Prick the bottoms of the pastry with a fork. Bake in the preheated oven for 10-12 minutes or until the tartlet shells are golden brown and puffed. Remove from the oven and let them cool.

Caramelized Onions:

Caramelize Onions:
- In a skillet, heat butter and olive oil over medium-low heat. Add thinly sliced onions, sugar, salt, and black pepper. Cook, stirring occasionally, until the onions are caramelized and golden brown. This may take around 20-30 minutes.

Optional Balsamic Reduction:
- If using, add balsamic vinegar to the caramelized onions and cook for an additional 2-3 minutes until the liquid is reduced. Remove from heat.

Assembly:

Fill Tartlet Shells:
- Preheat the oven to 375°F (190°C). Spoon a small amount of caramelized onions into each tartlet shell.

Add Gruyere Cheese:
- Top the caramelized onions with shredded Gruyere cheese.

Bake Again:
- Bake the tartlets in the preheated oven for about 8-10 minutes or until the cheese is melted and bubbly.

Garnish:
- Garnish the Caramelized Onion and Gruyere Tartlets with fresh thyme leaves.

Serve:
- Serve the tartlets warm as an appetizer or party snack.

Tips:

- Ensure that the puff pastry is thoroughly thawed but still cold for easy handling.
- Experiment with other cheese options like fontina or Swiss for different flavor profiles.
- You can make the tartlet shells and caramelized onions in advance and assemble them just before serving.

These Caramelized Onion and Gruyere Tartlets are a delightful combination of sweet caramelized onions, rich Gruyere cheese, and flaky puff pastry. Enjoy!

Coconut Shrimp with Mango Dipping Sauce

Ingredients:

For Coconut Shrimp:

- 1 pound large shrimp, peeled and deveined, tails intact
- 1 cup sweetened shredded coconut
- 1 cup Panko breadcrumbs
- 1/2 cup all-purpose flour
- 2 large eggs, beaten
- Salt and black pepper, to taste
- Vegetable oil for frying

For Mango Dipping Sauce:

- 1 ripe mango, peeled and diced
- 1/4 cup mayonnaise
- 1 tablespoon Dijon mustard
- 1 tablespoon honey
- 1 tablespoon lime juice
- 1 teaspoon Sriracha sauce (adjust to taste)
- Salt, to taste

Instructions:

Coconut Shrimp:

    Prepare Shrimp:
- Pat the shrimp dry with paper towels. Season with salt and black pepper.

    Set Up Breading Station:
- In three separate bowls, place flour in one, beaten eggs in another, and a mixture of sweetened shredded coconut and Panko breadcrumbs in the third.

    Bread the Shrimp:
- Dredge each shrimp in the flour, dip it into the beaten eggs, and then coat it thoroughly with the coconut-panko mixture, pressing gently to adhere. Place the breaded shrimp on a baking sheet.

    Chill (Optional):

- For extra crispiness, you can chill the breaded shrimp in the refrigerator for about 15-30 minutes.

Fry Shrimp:
- In a large skillet, heat vegetable oil over medium-high heat. Fry the coconut shrimp in batches for 2-3 minutes per side or until golden brown and crispy. Transfer to a paper towel-lined plate to drain excess oil.

Mango Dipping Sauce:

Blend Mango:
- In a blender or food processor, puree the diced mango until smooth.

Make Sauce:
- In a bowl, combine mango puree, mayonnaise, Dijon mustard, honey, lime juice, Sriracha sauce, and salt. Whisk until well combined.

Adjust Seasoning:
- Taste the mango dipping sauce and adjust the sweetness, acidity, or spiciness as needed.

Serve:

Plate:
- Arrange the Coconut Shrimp on a serving platter.

Dip and Enjoy:
- Serve the Coconut Shrimp with the Mango Dipping Sauce on the side. Enjoy the crispy, coconut-crusted goodness!

Tips:

- Adjust the level of sweetness in the dipping sauce by adding more or less honey.
- For a tropical twist, you can add a splash of coconut milk to the mango dipping sauce.
- Serve the coconut shrimp over a bed of mixed greens for a light and refreshing meal.

These Coconut Shrimp with Mango Dipping Sauce make for a delicious appetizer or a delightful addition to your seafood menu. Enjoy!

Tomato Basil Bruschetta

Ingredients:

- 4-5 ripe tomatoes, diced
- 1/2 cup fresh basil, finely chopped
- 3 cloves garlic, minced
- 2 tablespoons extra-virgin olive oil
- 1 teaspoon balsamic vinegar
- Salt and black pepper, to taste
- Baguette, sliced

Instructions:

Prepare Tomatoes:
- Dice the ripe tomatoes and place them in a bowl.

Add Basil and Garlic:
- Add finely chopped fresh basil and minced garlic to the diced tomatoes.

Season:
- Drizzle extra-virgin olive oil and balsamic vinegar over the tomato mixture. Season with salt and black pepper to taste.

Mix Well:
- Gently toss the ingredients together, ensuring the tomatoes are well coated with the oil, vinegar, and herbs.

Let it Marinate:
- Allow the bruschetta mixture to marinate for at least 15-20 minutes to let the flavors meld together. You can refrigerate it for a couple of hours for a more intense flavor.

Toast Baguette Slices:
- Preheat the oven or a toaster oven. Toast the baguette slices until they are golden and crispy.

Serve:
- Spoon the tomato basil mixture onto each toasted baguette slice.

Garnish (Optional):
- Garnish with additional fresh basil leaves if desired.

Enjoy:
- Serve the Tomato Basil Bruschetta immediately as an appetizer or a refreshing snack.

Tips:

- You can customize the bruschetta by adding ingredients like finely chopped red onion, diced bell peppers, or a sprinkle of feta cheese.
- For an extra kick, you can add a pinch of red pepper flakes or a drizzle of balsamic glaze.
- Use a crusty baguette or Italian bread for the best texture.

This Tomato Basil Bruschetta is a classic and simple appetizer that showcases the vibrant flavors of fresh tomatoes and basil. Enjoy!

Pigs in a Blanket with Dijon Mustard

Ingredients:

- Cocktail sausages or mini hot dogs
- Crescent roll dough (store-bought)
- Dijon mustard for dipping

Instructions:

Preheat Oven:
- Preheat your oven according to the crescent roll package instructions.

Prepare Dough:
- Roll out the crescent roll dough and separate it into individual triangles.

Cut Dough:
- If needed, cut each triangle into smaller triangles to better fit the size of your cocktail sausages or mini hot dogs.

Wrap Sausages:
- Place a cocktail sausage or mini hot dog at the wider end of each dough triangle. Roll the dough around the sausage, covering it completely.

Arrange on Baking Sheet:
- Place the wrapped sausages on a baking sheet lined with parchment paper, with the seam side down.

Bake:
- Bake in the preheated oven according to the crescent roll package instructions or until the dough is golden brown.

Serve:
- Remove from the oven and let them cool slightly. Serve the Pigs in a Blanket with Dijon Mustard on the side for dipping.

Tips:

- Experiment with different types of sausages or hot dogs to add variety.
- For an extra flavor boost, sprinkle some sesame seeds or poppy seeds on top of the wrapped sausages before baking.
- Ensure the crescent roll dough is sealed well to prevent the sausages from unraveling during baking.

These Pigs in a Blanket with Dijon Mustard make for a delicious and nostalgic appetizer, perfect for parties, game nights, or any casual gathering. Enjoy!

Avocado Egg Rolls with Sweet Chili Sauce

Ingredients:

For Avocado Egg Rolls:

- 2 ripe avocados, sliced
- 1/4 cup red onion, finely chopped
- 1/4 cup sun-dried tomatoes, chopped
- 1/4 cup cilantro, chopped
- 1 tablespoon lime juice
- Salt and black pepper, to taste
- Egg roll wrappers
- Vegetable oil for frying

For Sweet Chili Sauce:

- 1/2 cup sweet chili sauce
- 1 tablespoon soy sauce
- 1 teaspoon sesame oil

Instructions:

Avocado Egg Rolls:

> Prepare Avocado Filling:
> - In a bowl, combine sliced avocados, finely chopped red onion, sun-dried tomatoes, cilantro, lime juice, salt, and black pepper. Gently toss to combine.
>
> Assemble Egg Rolls:
> - Place an egg roll wrapper on a clean surface with one corner pointing toward you. Spoon a portion of the avocado filling onto the center of the wrapper.
>
> Fold and Seal:
> - Fold the bottom corner over the filling, then fold in the sides, and roll tightly. Use a dab of water on the edges to seal the egg roll.
>
> Repeat:
> - Repeat the process with the remaining wrappers and filling.
>
> Heat Oil:
> - In a large skillet or deep fryer, heat vegetable oil to 350°F (175°C).

Fry Egg Rolls:
- Carefully place the avocado egg rolls into the hot oil, a few at a time, and fry until they are golden brown and crispy. This usually takes about 2-3 minutes per side.

Drain and Cool:
- Remove the egg rolls with a slotted spoon and place them on a paper towel-lined plate to drain excess oil. Allow them to cool slightly.

Sweet Chili Sauce:

Prepare Sauce:
- In a small bowl, whisk together sweet chili sauce, soy sauce, and sesame oil.

Serve:

Plate:
- Arrange the Avocado Egg Rolls on a serving platter.

Dip and Enjoy:
- Serve with the Sweet Chili Sauce on the side for dipping. Enjoy the crunchy exterior and creamy avocado filling!

Tips:

- You can also bake the avocado egg rolls in the oven at 400°F (200°C) for about 15-20 minutes or until they are golden brown.
- Add a touch of spice to the avocado filling by incorporating a pinch of red pepper flakes or cayenne pepper.
- Customize the filling by adding ingredients like shredded cabbage, carrots, or cooked chicken for variation.

These Avocado Egg Rolls with Sweet Chili Sauce make for a tasty and satisfying appetizer, combining the richness of avocado with a crispy exterior. Enjoy!

Parmesan and Herb-Stuffed Cherry Tomatoes

Ingredients:

- Cherry tomatoes
- 1/2 cup cream cheese, softened
- 1/4 cup grated Parmesan cheese
- 2 tablespoons fresh herbs (such as basil, parsley, or chives), finely chopped
- Salt and black pepper, to taste
- Olive oil for drizzling (optional)

Instructions:

Prepare Cherry Tomatoes:
- Cut a small slice off the bottom of each cherry tomato so that they can stand upright.

Hollow Out Tomatoes:
- Using a small spoon or a melon baller, carefully hollow out the center of each cherry tomato. Discard the seeds and excess pulp.

Prepare Filling:
- In a bowl, combine softened cream cheese, grated Parmesan cheese, finely chopped fresh herbs, salt, and black pepper. Mix until well combined.

Fill Tomatoes:
- Using a small spoon or a piping bag, fill each hollowed cherry tomato with the cream cheese mixture. Smooth the tops with the back of the spoon.

Chill (Optional):
- If time allows, chill the stuffed cherry tomatoes in the refrigerator for at least 30 minutes to allow the flavors to meld.

Drizzle with Olive Oil (Optional):
- Just before serving, drizzle the stuffed cherry tomatoes with a bit of olive oil for added richness and flavor.

Serve:
- Arrange the Parmesan and Herb-Stuffed Cherry Tomatoes on a serving platter and serve as an elegant and flavorful appetizer.

Tips:

- Experiment with different herb combinations to suit your taste preferences.

- You can add a dash of garlic powder or minced garlic to the cream cheese mixture for extra flavor.
- Garnish with additional fresh herbs or a sprinkle of Parmesan cheese before serving.

These Parmesan and Herb-Stuffed Cherry Tomatoes are a delightful and visually appealing appetizer that's perfect for parties, gatherings, or as a light snack. Enjoy!

Buffalo Cauliflower Bites

Ingredients:

For Buffalo Cauliflower:

- 1 medium-sized cauliflower, cut into florets
- 1 cup all-purpose flour
- 1 cup milk (or plant-based milk for a vegan option)
- 1 teaspoon garlic powder
- 1 teaspoon onion powder
- 1/2 teaspoon smoked paprika
- Salt and black pepper, to taste
- 1 cup buffalo sauce
- 1/4 cup unsalted butter (or vegan butter for a vegan option), melted

For Serving:

- Celery sticks
- Carrot sticks
- Ranch dressing or blue cheese dressing for dipping

Instructions:

Preheat Oven:
- Preheat your oven to 450°F (230°C).

Prepare Cauliflower:
- Cut the cauliflower into bite-sized florets.

Make Batter:
- In a bowl, whisk together the flour, milk, garlic powder, onion powder, smoked paprika, salt, and black pepper to create a smooth batter.

Coat Cauliflower:
- Dip each cauliflower floret into the batter, ensuring it is well-coated, and shake off any excess.

Bake:
- Place the battered cauliflower on a baking sheet lined with parchment paper. Bake in the preheated oven for 20-25 minutes or until the cauliflower is golden and crispy.

Prepare Buffalo Sauce:

- While the cauliflower is baking, mix the melted butter and buffalo sauce in a bowl.

Toss in Buffalo Sauce:
- Once the cauliflower is done, transfer it to a large mixing bowl. Pour the buffalo sauce mixture over the cauliflower and toss until the pieces are evenly coated.

Serve:
- Serve the Buffalo Cauliflower Bites with celery and carrot sticks on the side. Add ranch dressing or blue cheese dressing for dipping.

Tips:

- Adjust the level of spiciness by adding more or less buffalo sauce according to your taste preferences.
- For extra crispiness, you can place a wire rack on the baking sheet before arranging the battered cauliflower.
- Feel free to experiment with different seasonings in the batter for added flavor.

These Buffalo Cauliflower Bites are a tasty and healthier alternative to traditional buffalo wings, perfect for vegetarians or anyone looking for a flavorful appetizer. Enjoy!

Cheese and Herb-Stuffed Puff Pastry Twists

Ingredients:

- 1 sheet of puff pastry, thawed if frozen
- 1 cup shredded cheese (cheddar, mozzarella, or your choice)
- 2 tablespoons fresh herbs (such as parsley, thyme, or chives), finely chopped
- 1/4 cup grated Parmesan cheese
- 1 egg (for egg wash)
- Salt and black pepper, to taste
- Optional: Garlic powder or minced garlic for extra flavor

Instructions:

Preheat Oven:
- Preheat your oven to 400°F (200°C).

Roll Out Puff Pastry:
- On a lightly floured surface, roll out the puff pastry sheet.

Add Cheese and Herbs:
- Sprinkle the shredded cheese evenly over the puff pastry. Next, sprinkle the fresh herbs, grated Parmesan cheese, and season with salt and black pepper. Optionally, you can add a touch of garlic powder or minced garlic for extra flavor.

Fold and Press:
- Gently fold the puff pastry in half to cover the cheese and herbs. Press down lightly to seal the edges.

Cut into Strips:
- Using a sharp knife or a pizza cutter, cut the puff pastry into strips, about 1/2 to 1 inch wide.

Twist the Strips:
- Take each strip and gently twist it from one end to the other. Place the twisted strips on a baking sheet lined with parchment paper.

Prepare Egg Wash:
- In a small bowl, beat the egg to create an egg wash.

Brush with Egg Wash:
- Brush the twisted puff pastry strips with the egg wash, ensuring they are well-coated for a golden finish.

Bake:

- Bake in the preheated oven for 12-15 minutes or until the Cheese and Herb-Stuffed Puff Pastry Twists are puffed up and golden brown.

Cool and Serve:
- Allow the twists to cool slightly before serving. They can be enjoyed warm or at room temperature.

Tips:

- Customize the cheese and herb filling with your favorite combinations. Consider adding a sprinkle of red pepper flakes for a hint of spice.
- Experiment with different herbs, such as rosemary, oregano, or basil, to suit your taste.
- Serve with a side of marinara sauce or a yogurt-based dipping sauce for extra enjoyment.

These Cheese and Herb-Stuffed Puff Pastry Twists are a delightful and easy-to-make appetizer or snack that's perfect for entertaining. Enjoy!

Crispy Zucchini Fries with Garlic Aioli

Ingredients:

For Zucchini Fries:

- 2 medium zucchinis, cut into fries
- 1 cup panko breadcrumbs
- 1/2 cup grated Parmesan cheese
- 1 teaspoon garlic powder
- 1 teaspoon onion powder
- 1/2 teaspoon smoked paprika
- Salt and black pepper, to taste
- 2 large eggs, beaten
- Cooking spray or olive oil for greasing

For Garlic Aioli:

- 1/2 cup mayonnaise
- 2 cloves garlic, minced
- 1 tablespoon lemon juice
- Salt and black pepper, to taste

Instructions:

Zucchini Fries:

    Preheat Oven:
- Preheat your oven to 425°F (220°C). Line a baking sheet with parchment paper and lightly grease it with cooking spray or olive oil.

    Prepare Zucchini:
- Cut the zucchinis into fry-shaped sticks.

    Create Breadcrumb Mixture:
- In a bowl, combine panko breadcrumbs, grated Parmesan cheese, garlic powder, onion powder, smoked paprika, salt, and black pepper.

    Coat Zucchini:
- Dip each zucchini fry into the beaten eggs, ensuring it's fully coated. Then, coat the zucchini with the breadcrumb mixture, pressing gently to adhere the crumbs.

    Arrange on Baking Sheet:

- Place the coated zucchini fries on the prepared baking sheet in a single layer, leaving space between each fry.

Bake:
- Bake in the preheated oven for 20-25 minutes or until the zucchini fries are golden brown and crispy. Flip them halfway through the baking time for even crispiness.

Garlic Aioli:

Prepare Aioli:
- In a small bowl, mix together mayonnaise, minced garlic, lemon juice, salt, and black pepper. Adjust seasoning to taste.

Chill (Optional):
- If time allows, chill the garlic aioli in the refrigerator for at least 15-20 minutes to allow the flavors to meld.

Serve:

Plate:
- Arrange the Crispy Zucchini Fries on a serving platter.

Dip and Enjoy:
- Serve with the Garlic Aioli on the side for dipping. Enjoy the crispy goodness!

Tips:

- For extra crispiness, you can place a wire rack on the baking sheet to elevate the zucchini fries during baking.
- Experiment with different seasonings in the breadcrumb mixture, such as dried herbs or a pinch of cayenne pepper.
- Customize the garlic aioli by adding a touch of Dijon mustard or fresh herbs for additional flavor.

These Crispy Zucchini Fries with Garlic Aioli make for a delicious and healthier alternative to traditional fries, perfect for snacking or as a side dish. Enjoy!

Lobster and Avocado Wonton Cups

Ingredients:

For Wonton Cups:

- Wonton wrappers
- Cooking spray or olive oil for greasing

For Lobster and Avocado Filling:

- 1 cup cooked lobster meat, chopped
- 2 ripe avocados, diced
- 1/4 cup red onion, finely chopped
- 2 tablespoons fresh cilantro, chopped
- 1 tablespoon lime juice
- Salt and black pepper, to taste

For Garnish:

- Fresh cilantro leaves
- Lime wedges

Instructions:

Wonton Cups:

    Preheat Oven:
- Preheat your oven to 350°F (175°C).

    Shape Wonton Cups:
- Lightly spray a mini muffin tin with cooking spray. Gently press wonton wrappers into the cups of the muffin tin, forming small cups.

    Bake:
- Bake in the preheated oven for 8-10 minutes or until the wonton cups are golden and crisp. Keep an eye on them to prevent burning.

    Cool:
- Allow the wonton cups to cool in the muffin tin for a few minutes before transferring them to a wire rack to cool completely.

Lobster and Avocado Filling:

Prepare Lobster:
- If you haven't done so already, cook and chop the lobster meat. You can use pre-cooked lobster or cook it according to your preferred method.

Combine Ingredients:
- In a bowl, combine chopped lobster meat, diced avocados, finely chopped red onion, chopped cilantro, lime juice, salt, and black pepper. Gently toss the ingredients together.

Assemble:

Fill Wonton Cups:
- Spoon the lobster and avocado mixture into each cooled wonton cup.

Garnish:
- Garnish each Lobster and Avocado Wonton Cup with fresh cilantro leaves and serve with lime wedges on the side.

Tips:

- To prevent the wonton cups from getting soggy, assemble them shortly before serving.
- You can add a kick of heat by incorporating a small amount of minced jalapeño or a pinch of red pepper flakes into the lobster and avocado mixture.
- Experiment with different herbs or add a drizzle of your favorite dressing for extra flavor.

These Lobster and Avocado Wonton Cups make for an elegant and flavorful appetizer, perfect for special occasions or gatherings. Enjoy!

Smoky Chipotle Meatballs

Ingredients:

For Meatballs:

- 1 pound ground beef (or a mix of ground beef and pork)
- 1/2 cup breadcrumbs
- 1/4 cup grated Parmesan cheese
- 2 cloves garlic, minced
- 1/4 cup fresh parsley, finely chopped
- 1 large egg
- 1 teaspoon smoked paprika
- 1 teaspoon dried oregano
- Salt and black pepper, to taste
- Cooking spray or olive oil for greasing

For Chipotle Sauce:

- 1 cup tomato sauce
- 2 chipotle peppers in adobo sauce, minced
- 1 tablespoon adobo sauce (from the chipotle pepper can)
- 1 tablespoon honey or brown sugar
- 1 teaspoon ground cumin
- Salt, to taste

For Garnish:

- Fresh cilantro, chopped
- Lime wedges

Instructions:

Meatballs:

    Preheat Oven:
- Preheat your oven to 375°F (190°C).

    Prepare Meatball Mixture:

- In a large bowl, combine ground beef, breadcrumbs, grated Parmesan cheese, minced garlic, chopped parsley, egg, smoked paprika, dried oregano, salt, and black pepper. Mix until well combined.

Shape Meatballs:
- Shape the mixture into meatballs, approximately 1 inch in diameter, and place them on a baking sheet lined with parchment paper. You should get about 20-24 meatballs.

Bake:
- Bake in the preheated oven for 20-25 minutes or until the meatballs are cooked through and browned on the outside.

Chipotle Sauce:

Prepare Sauce:
- In a saucepan, combine tomato sauce, minced chipotle peppers, adobo sauce, honey (or brown sugar), ground cumin, and salt. Simmer over low heat for 10-15 minutes, allowing the flavors to meld.

Assembly:

Toss Meatballs in Sauce:
- Once the meatballs are cooked, toss them in the chipotle sauce, ensuring they are well coated.

Garnish:
- Garnish the Smoky Chipotle Meatballs with chopped fresh cilantro and serve with lime wedges on the side.

Tips:

- Adjust the level of spiciness by adding more or fewer chipotle peppers.
- If you prefer a smoother sauce, you can use a blender or immersion blender to puree the chipotle sauce.
- Serve the meatballs as an appetizer with toothpicks or as a main dish over rice or pasta.

These Smoky Chipotle Meatballs offer a perfect blend of smokiness, spice, and savory goodness. Enjoy them as a delicious appetizer or as part of a flavorful meal!

Edamame and Ginger Potstickers

Ingredients:

For Potstickers:

- 1 cup shelled edamame, cooked
- 1 cup cabbage, finely chopped
- 2 green onions, finely chopped
- 2 cloves garlic, minced
- 1 tablespoon fresh ginger, grated
- 1 tablespoon soy sauce
- 1 teaspoon sesame oil
- 1 package round potsticker or gyoza wrappers
- Water (for sealing wrappers)
- Cooking oil (vegetable or sesame oil) for pan-frying

For Dipping Sauce:

- 1/4 cup soy sauce
- 1 tablespoon rice vinegar
- 1 teaspoon sesame oil
- 1 teaspoon honey or maple syrup (optional)
- 1 teaspoon fresh ginger, grated (optional)
- Red pepper flakes (optional, for added spice)

Instructions:

Filling:

> Prepare Edamame:
> - Cook the shelled edamame according to the package instructions. Drain and set aside.
>
> Mash Edamame:
> - In a bowl, mash the cooked edamame using a fork or potato masher.
>
> Mix Filling:
> - Combine the mashed edamame, chopped cabbage, green onions, minced garlic, grated ginger, soy sauce, and sesame oil in a bowl. Mix well to create the potsticker filling.

Assembly:

Wrap Potstickers:
- Place a small amount of the filling in the center of a potsticker wrapper. Moisten the edge of the wrapper with water, fold in half, and pinch the edges to seal, creating a half-moon shape. Repeat with the remaining wrappers and filling.

Crimp Edges:
- Optionally, crimp the edges of the potstickers for a decorative touch.

Cooking:

Pan-Fry Potstickers:
- Heat cooking oil in a large skillet over medium-high heat. Place the potstickers in the skillet, ensuring they are not touching each other. Cook until the bottoms are golden brown.

Steam and Crisp:
- Pour a small amount of water into the skillet and cover immediately to steam the potstickers. Reduce heat to medium and cook for an additional 5-7 minutes until the wrappers are translucent and the filling is cooked through. Uncover and let the potstickers crisp up on the bottom.

Dipping Sauce:

Prepare Sauce:
- In a small bowl, mix soy sauce, rice vinegar, sesame oil, honey (or maple syrup), and grated ginger for the dipping sauce. Adjust the ingredients to taste. Add red pepper flakes for extra spice if desired.

Serve:

Plate:
- Arrange the Edamame and Ginger Potstickers on a serving platter.

Dip and Enjoy:
- Serve the potstickers with the dipping sauce on the side. Enjoy these flavorful and satisfying dumplings!

Tips:

- You can find round potsticker or gyoza wrappers in the refrigerated section of most grocery stores or at Asian markets.
- Make sure to keep the potstickers from touching each other while cooking to prevent them from sticking together.
- Double the batch and freeze uncooked potstickers for a quick and delicious snack or meal later on.

These Edamame and Ginger Potstickers are a delightful fusion of flavors and textures, making them a tasty appetizer or a main dish. Enjoy!

Sesame Ginger Chicken Lettuce Wraps

Ingredients:

For Chicken Filling:

- 1 pound ground chicken
- 2 tablespoons sesame oil
- 3 cloves garlic, minced
- 1 tablespoon fresh ginger, grated
- 1/4 cup soy sauce
- 2 tablespoons hoisin sauce
- 1 tablespoon rice vinegar
- 1 tablespoon honey
- 1 teaspoon Sriracha sauce (optional, for heat)
- 1/4 cup green onions, chopped
- 1 tablespoon sesame seeds (for garnish)

For Lettuce Wraps:

- Large lettuce leaves (such as iceberg or butter lettuce)
- Shredded carrots
- Bean sprouts
- Additional chopped green onions for garnish

Instructions:

Chicken Filling:

Cook Chicken:
- In a large skillet or wok, heat sesame oil over medium-high heat. Add ground chicken and cook until browned and cooked through.

Add Aromatics:
- Add minced garlic and grated ginger to the cooked chicken. Sauté for 1-2 minutes until fragrant.

Sauce Mixture:
- In a bowl, mix soy sauce, hoisin sauce, rice vinegar, honey, and Sriracha sauce (if using). Pour the sauce mixture over the chicken.

Combine and Simmer:

- Stir to coat the chicken in the sauce. Allow the mixture to simmer for 3-5 minutes, allowing the flavors to meld and the sauce to thicken slightly.

Add Green Onions:
- Add chopped green onions to the chicken mixture and cook for an additional 1-2 minutes.

Garnish:
- Sprinkle sesame seeds over the chicken as a garnish. Stir to combine.

Assemble Lettuce Wraps:

Prepare Lettuce Leaves:
- Wash and separate large lettuce leaves. Pat them dry with paper towels.

Fill Lettuce Leaves:
- Spoon the sesame ginger chicken mixture into the center of each lettuce leaf.

Add Toppings:
- Top the chicken with shredded carrots, bean sprouts, and additional chopped green onions.

Roll and Serve:
- Roll the lettuce leaves around the filling, creating a wrap. Secure with toothpicks if needed.

Serve:

Plate:
- Arrange the Sesame Ginger Chicken Lettuce Wraps on a serving platter.

Garnish and Enjoy:
- Garnish with extra sesame seeds and serve immediately. Enjoy these flavorful and refreshing lettuce wraps!

Tips:

- Customize the level of spiciness by adjusting the amount of Sriracha sauce or by adding red pepper flakes.
- For added crunch, sprinkle crushed peanuts or water chestnuts over the chicken filling.
- Drizzle extra hoisin sauce or a squeeze of lime juice over the assembled wraps for additional flavor.

These Sesame Ginger Chicken Lettuce Wraps make for a light and satisfying meal or appetizer. The combination of savory, sweet, and nutty flavors creates a delightful eating experience. Enjoy!

Roasted Red Pepper and Walnut Dip (Muhammara)

Ingredients:

- 2 large red bell peppers, roasted and peeled
- 1 cup walnuts, toasted
- 2 cloves garlic, minced
- 1 tablespoon tomato paste
- 1 tablespoon pomegranate molasses
- 1 teaspoon ground cumin
- 1 teaspoon smoked paprika
- 1/2 teaspoon red pepper flakes (adjust to taste)
- Salt and black pepper, to taste
- 3 tablespoons extra-virgin olive oil
- Fresh parsley, chopped (for garnish)
- Pomegranate arils (for garnish, optional)

Instructions:

Roast Red Peppers:
- Preheat the oven broiler. Place red bell peppers on a baking sheet and broil, turning occasionally, until the skin is charred and blistered. Remove from the oven, place in a bowl, and cover with plastic wrap. Allow them to steam for about 10 minutes. Peel off the skin, remove seeds, and chop the roasted peppers.

Toast Walnuts:
- In a dry skillet over medium heat, toast the walnuts until they are fragrant. Be careful not to burn them. Remove from the heat and let them cool.

Prepare Dip:
- In a food processor, combine the roasted red peppers, toasted walnuts, minced garlic, tomato paste, pomegranate molasses, ground cumin, smoked paprika, red pepper flakes, salt, and black pepper.

Blend:
- Pulse the ingredients until well combined. While the food processor is running, gradually add the olive oil in a steady stream until the mixture becomes smooth and creamy.

Adjust Seasoning:
- Taste and adjust the seasoning, adding more salt, pepper, or red pepper flakes if needed.

Serve:
- Transfer the Muhammara to a serving bowl. Drizzle with extra olive oil, and garnish with chopped fresh parsley and optional pomegranate arils.

Chill (Optional):
- For enhanced flavors, refrigerate the dip for at least 1-2 hours before serving.

Enjoy:
- Serve Muhammara with pita bread, crackers, or vegetable sticks. Enjoy as a flavorful dip or spread.

Tips:

- Adjust the consistency by adding more olive oil if you prefer a smoother or thinner dip.
- If pomegranate molasses is not available, you can substitute it with balsamic glaze or honey for a touch of sweetness.
- Customize the level of spiciness by adjusting the amount of red pepper flakes.
- Muhammara can be stored in an airtight container in the refrigerator for several days.

This Roasted Red Pepper and Walnut Dip (Muhammara) is a delicious and versatile appetizer that brings a unique combination of flavors to your table. Enjoy the rich and nutty goodness!

Spicy Mango Salsa with Tortilla Chips

Ingredients:

- 2 ripe mangoes, diced
- 1 cup cherry tomatoes, halved
- 1/2 red onion, finely chopped
- 1 jalapeño pepper, seeds removed and finely diced
- 1/4 cup fresh cilantro, chopped
- Juice of 2 limes
- 1 tablespoon olive oil
- Salt and black pepper, to taste
- 1 teaspoon honey (optional, for sweetness)
- Tortilla chips, for serving

Instructions:

Prepare Ingredients:
- Peel and dice the ripe mangoes. Halve the cherry tomatoes. Finely chop the red onion. Dice the jalapeño pepper, removing the seeds for less heat if desired. Chop fresh cilantro.

Combine Ingredients:
- In a large bowl, combine the diced mangoes, halved cherry tomatoes, chopped red onion, diced jalapeño pepper, and chopped cilantro.

Make Dressing:
- In a small bowl, whisk together the lime juice, olive oil, salt, black pepper, and honey (if using). Adjust the sweetness and seasoning to taste.

Toss and Chill:
- Pour the dressing over the mango salsa ingredients. Gently toss everything together until well combined. Allow the salsa to chill in the refrigerator for at least 30 minutes to let the flavors meld.

Serve:
- Just before serving, give the Spicy Mango Salsa a final toss. Serve it in a bowl alongside your favorite tortilla chips.

Tips:

- Adjust the level of spiciness by adding more or less jalapeño pepper, or leave the seeds in for extra heat.
- If you prefer a sweeter salsa, increase the amount of honey to your liking.
- Experiment with additional ingredients such as diced avocado or cucumber for added freshness and texture.
- This salsa can be served as a topping for grilled chicken, fish, or tacos.

This Spicy Mango Salsa with Tortilla Chips is a refreshing and vibrant snack or appetizer that combines the sweetness of mangoes with the kick of jalapeño. Enjoy the tropical flavors!

Crispy Polenta Bites with Gorgonzola

Ingredients:

For Crispy Polenta:

- 1 cup instant polenta
- 4 cups water
- 1 teaspoon salt
- 1/2 cup grated Parmesan cheese
- 2 tablespoons unsalted butter
- Cooking spray or olive oil for greasing

For Topping:

- 1/2 cup Gorgonzola cheese, crumbled
- Honey, for drizzling
- Fresh thyme leaves, for garnish

Instructions:

Crispy Polenta:

Cook Polenta:
- In a saucepan, bring 4 cups of water to a boil. Add salt and gradually whisk in instant polenta. Reduce heat to low and continue whisking for 2-3 minutes until the polenta thickens.

Add Cheese and Butter:

- Remove from heat and stir in grated Parmesan cheese and unsalted butter until well combined.

Spread in Pan:

- Grease a square or rectangular baking dish with cooking spray or olive oil. Spread the polenta evenly in the dish and smooth the surface.

Chill:

- Allow the polenta to cool and set in the refrigerator for at least 1-2 hours, or until firm.

Cut into Bites:

- Once the polenta is firm, cut it into bite-sized squares or rectangles.

Bake:

- Preheat your oven to 400°F (200°C). Place the polenta bites on a baking sheet lined with parchment paper. Bake for 20-25 minutes or until the edges are crispy and golden.

Assembly:

Top with Gorgonzola:

- Remove the crispy polenta bites from the oven and immediately sprinkle crumbled Gorgonzola cheese on top of each bite.

Drizzle with Honey:

- Drizzle honey over the Gorgonzola-topped polenta bites for a sweet contrast.

Garnish:

- Garnish with fresh thyme leaves for added flavor and presentation.

Serve Warm:

- Serve the Crispy Polenta Bites with Gorgonzola warm as an elegant and flavorful appetizer.

Tips:

- Customize the toppings by adding chopped nuts (such as walnuts or pine nuts) or a balsamic reduction for extra flavor.
- Experiment with different types of cheese for a variety of flavor profiles.
- Serve these bites with a side of arugula or mixed greens for a balanced presentation.

These Crispy Polenta Bites with Gorgonzola are a delightful combination of creamy polenta, crispy edges, tangy Gorgonzola, and sweet honey. They make for an impressive appetizer that's easy to prepare. Enjoy!

Chorizo-Stuffed Mushrooms

Ingredients:

- 24 large mushrooms, cleaned and stems removed
- 1/2 pound (about 225g) chorizo sausage, casing removed and finely chopped
- 1/2 cup breadcrumbs
- 1/2 cup shredded Manchego or Monterey Jack cheese
- 1/4 cup finely chopped onion
- 2 cloves garlic, minced
- 2 tablespoons fresh parsley, chopped
- 2 tablespoons olive oil
- Salt and black pepper, to taste
- Smoked paprika, for garnish (optional)
- Fresh parsley, for garnish

Instructions:

Preheat Oven:

- Preheat your oven to 375°F (190°C).

Prepare Mushrooms:

- Clean the mushrooms and remove the stems. Place the mushroom caps on a baking sheet, cap side down.

Prepare Filling:

- In a skillet, heat olive oil over medium heat. Add chopped chorizo and cook until browned and cooked through. Remove any excess grease.

Combine Ingredients:

- In a bowl, combine the cooked chorizo, breadcrumbs, shredded cheese, chopped onion, minced garlic, and fresh parsley. Mix well. Season with salt and black pepper to taste.

Stuff Mushrooms:

- Spoon the chorizo mixture into each mushroom cap, pressing it down gently to ensure it's packed.

Bake:

- Bake in the preheated oven for 20-25 minutes or until the mushrooms are tender and the filling is golden brown.

Garnish:

- If desired, sprinkle smoked paprika for additional flavor and garnish with fresh parsley.

Serve:

- Serve the Chorizo-Stuffed Mushrooms warm as an appetizer or party snack.

Tips:

- Adjust the level of spiciness by choosing mild or spicy chorizo according to your preference.
- Experiment with different cheese options for varied flavors. Manchego, Monterey Jack, or even cheddar work well.
- You can prepare the stuffed mushrooms in advance and bake them just before serving for a convenient party appetizer.

These Chorizo-Stuffed Mushrooms are a flavorful and savory appetizer, perfect for entertaining or as a delicious snack. Enjoy!

Sun-Dried Tomato and Basil Pinwheels

Ingredients:

- 1 sheet puff pastry, thawed
- 1/2 cup sun-dried tomatoes (packed in oil), drained and finely chopped
- 1/4 cup fresh basil leaves, chopped
- 1/2 cup cream cheese, softened
- 1/4 cup grated Parmesan cheese
- 1 clove garlic, minced
- Salt and black pepper, to taste
- 1 egg, beaten (for egg wash)

Instructions:

Preheat Oven:

- Preheat your oven to 375°F (190°C).

Prepare Puff Pastry:

- Roll out the thawed puff pastry on a lightly floured surface to create a rectangle.

Mix Filling:

- In a bowl, mix together the cream cheese, chopped sun-dried tomatoes, fresh basil, grated Parmesan cheese, minced garlic, salt, and black pepper.

Spread Filling:

- Spread the cream cheese mixture evenly over the entire surface of the puff pastry.

Roll into a Log:

- Starting from one edge, tightly roll the puff pastry into a log or cylinder shape.

Chill (Optional):
- If time allows, you can place the rolled log in the refrigerator for about 15-20 minutes to make it easier to slice.

Slice into Pinwheels:
- Using a sharp knife, slice the rolled puff pastry into 1/2-inch thick pinwheels.

Place on Baking Sheet:
- Place the pinwheels on a baking sheet lined with parchment paper, leaving space between each.

Brush with Egg Wash:
- Brush the tops of the pinwheels with the beaten egg to give them a golden finish when baked.

Bake:
- Bake in the preheated oven for 15-20 minutes or until the pinwheels are puffed and golden.

Serve:
- Allow the Sun-Dried Tomato and Basil Pinwheels to cool slightly before serving. They can be served warm or at room temperature.

Tips:

- Customize the filling by adding chopped olives, roasted red peppers, or a sprinkle of red pepper flakes for extra flavor.
- Experiment with different herbs and cheeses to suit your taste preferences.

- Serve these pinwheels as appetizers for parties, gatherings, or as a tasty snack.

These Sun-Dried Tomato and Basil Pinwheels are not only visually appealing but also bursting with savory flavors. Enjoy the delightful combination of sun-dried tomatoes, basil, and creamy cheese in each bite!

Cucumber Cups with Crab Salad

Ingredients:

For Cucumber Cups:

- 2 large English cucumbers
- Salt (for sprinkling)

For Crab Salad:

- 1 cup lump crab meat, cooked and shredded
- 1/4 cup mayonnaise
- 1 tablespoon Greek yogurt or sour cream
- 1 teaspoon Dijon mustard
- 1 green onion, finely chopped
- 1 tablespoon fresh dill, chopped
- 1 teaspoon lemon juice
- Salt and black pepper, to taste

For Garnish (Optional):

- Fresh dill sprigs
- Lemon wedges

Instructions:

Cucumber Cups:

    Prepare Cucumbers:

- Wash the cucumbers and cut them into 2-inch thick rounds. Scoop out the seeds from the center of each round, leaving a well to create the cucumber cups.

Sprinkle with Salt:

- Lightly sprinkle the cucumber cups with salt and let them sit for about 10-15 minutes to draw out excess moisture. This step helps keep the cups crisp.

Pat Dry:

- Pat the cucumber cups dry with a paper towel to remove any released moisture.

Crab Salad:

Prepare Crab Salad:

- In a bowl, combine the cooked and shredded lump crab meat with mayonnaise, Greek yogurt (or sour cream), Dijon mustard, chopped green onion, chopped fresh dill, lemon juice, salt, and black pepper. Mix well to combine.

Adjust Seasoning:

- Taste the crab salad and adjust the seasoning, adding more salt, pepper, or lemon juice if needed.

Assemble:

Fill Cucumber Cups:

- Spoon the crab salad mixture into the well of each cucumber cup, filling them generously.

Garnish (Optional):

- Garnish each Cucumber Cup with Crab Salad with a sprig of fresh dill and serve with lemon wedges on the side.

Serve:

- Arrange the cucumber cups on a serving platter and serve immediately as a refreshing and elegant appetizer.

Tips:

- Be cautious with the salt, as both the crab meat and mayonnaise may already contain salt. Adjust the seasoning to your preference.
- If you prefer a spicier kick, add a pinch of cayenne pepper or a dash of hot sauce to the crab salad.
- For a different twist, consider adding diced avocado or mango to the crab salad for added flavor and texture.

These Cucumber Cups with Crab Salad are not only visually appealing but also a light and flavorful appetizer. They are perfect for summer gatherings or any occasion where you want to impress with a refreshing dish. Enjoy!

Pesto and Sun-Dried Tomato Cheese Ball

Ingredients:

- 8 oz (about 225g) cream cheese, softened
- 1/2 cup shredded mozzarella cheese
- 1/4 cup grated Parmesan cheese
- 1/4 cup sun-dried tomatoes, finely chopped
- 2 tablespoons pesto sauce
- 1 clove garlic, minced
- 1/4 teaspoon black pepper
- 1/4 cup fresh basil, finely chopped (for coating)
- 1/4 cup chopped nuts (such as pine nuts or almonds), toasted (for coating)

Instructions:

Prepare Cheese Mixture:

- In a mixing bowl, combine softened cream cheese, shredded mozzarella, grated Parmesan, finely chopped sun-dried tomatoes, pesto sauce, minced garlic, and black pepper. Mix until well combined.

Shape into a Ball:

- Shape the cheese mixture into a ball using your hands. If the mixture is too soft, you can refrigerate it for about 30 minutes to make it easier to handle.

Prepare Coating:

- On a plate or shallow dish, combine finely chopped fresh basil and toasted chopped nuts.

Roll in Coating:

- Roll the cheese ball in the basil and nut mixture, ensuring it is evenly coated on all sides.

Chill (Optional):

- For enhanced flavor, you can refrigerate the Pesto and Sun-Dried Tomato Cheese Ball for at least 1-2 hours before serving.

Serve:

- Place the cheese ball on a serving platter and serve with crackers, bread, or vegetable sticks.

Tips:

- Customize the nut coating based on your preference. You can use different nuts or a combination of nuts for added texture and flavor.
- If you don't have pre-made pesto, you can make a simple basil pesto by blending fresh basil, garlic, pine nuts, Parmesan cheese, and olive oil in a food processor.
- For an extra kick, add a pinch of red pepper flakes or cayenne pepper to the cheese mixture.

This Pesto and Sun-Dried Tomato Cheese Ball is a crowd-pleasing appetizer that combines the rich flavors of pesto and sun-dried tomatoes. It's perfect for entertaining and adds a touch of elegance to any gathering. Enjoy!

Mango Habanero Glazed Meatballs

Ingredients:

For Meatballs:

- 1 pound ground meat (beef, pork, chicken, or a mix)
- 1/2 cup breadcrumbs
- 1/4 cup finely chopped onion
- 2 cloves garlic, minced
- 1 egg
- 1 tablespoon soy sauce
- Salt and black pepper, to taste
- Cooking spray or olive oil for greasing

For Mango Habanero Glaze:

- 1 cup mango puree (fresh or canned)
- 2 habanero peppers, seeds removed and finely chopped
- 1/4 cup brown sugar
- 2 tablespoons rice vinegar
- 1 tablespoon soy sauce
- 1 teaspoon fresh ginger, grated
- 1 clove garlic, minced

For Garnish (Optional):

- Sesame seeds

- Chopped green onions
- Fresh cilantro, chopped

Instructions:

Meatballs:

Preheat Oven:
- Preheat your oven to 375°F (190°C).

Prepare Meatball Mixture:
- In a bowl, combine ground meat, breadcrumbs, chopped onion, minced garlic, egg, soy sauce, salt, and black pepper. Mix until well combined.

Shape Meatballs:
- Shape the mixture into meatballs, approximately 1 inch in diameter, and place them on a baking sheet lined with parchment paper. You should get about 20-24 meatballs.

Bake:
- Bake in the preheated oven for 20-25 minutes or until the meatballs are cooked through and browned on the outside.

Mango Habanero Glaze:

Prepare Glaze:
- In a saucepan, combine mango puree, finely chopped habanero peppers, brown sugar, rice vinegar, soy sauce, grated ginger, and minced garlic.

Simmer:
- Bring the mixture to a simmer over medium heat, stirring occasionally. Allow it to simmer for 10-15 minutes until the glaze thickens slightly.

Adjust Heat:

- Taste the glaze and adjust the heat by adding more habanero if you want it spicier or a bit more brown sugar for sweetness.

Assembly:

Coat Meatballs:

- Once the meatballs are cooked, toss them in the mango habanero glaze until they are well coated.

Serve:

- Arrange the Mango Habanero Glazed Meatballs on a serving platter. Garnish with sesame seeds, chopped green onions, and fresh cilantro if desired.

Tips:

- Adjust the level of spiciness by adding more or fewer habanero peppers. Be cautious, as habaneros are very spicy.
- If fresh mangoes are not available, you can use canned mango puree or frozen mango chunks for the glaze.
- Serve the meatballs with toothpicks as an appetizer, or over rice as a delicious main dish.

These Mango Habanero Glazed Meatballs are a perfect blend of sweet and spicy, making them a delightful and flavorful appetizer or main course. Enjoy the burst of tropical flavors!

Feta and Spinach Stuffed Phyllo Cups

Ingredients:

For Phyllo Cups:

- 1 package (about 15 sheets) phyllo dough, thawed
- 1/2 cup unsalted butter, melted
- Cooking spray

For Feta and Spinach Filling:

- 2 cups fresh spinach, chopped
- 1 cup feta cheese, crumbled
- 1/4 cup ricotta cheese
- 1/4 cup grated Parmesan cheese
- 1 clove garlic, minced
- 1 green onion, finely chopped
- 1 tablespoon olive oil
- Salt and black pepper, to taste
- Pinch of nutmeg (optional)

Instructions:

Phyllo Cups:

    Preheat Oven:

- Preheat your oven to 350°F (175°C).

    Prepare Phyllo Dough:

- Lay out one sheet of phyllo dough and brush it lightly with melted butter. Place another sheet on top and repeat until you have a stack of 5 sheets.

Cut Phyllo Stack:

- Cut the stack into squares or rectangles, depending on the size of your muffin tin.

Assemble Cups:

- Lightly coat each cup of a muffin tin with cooking spray. Press each phyllo stack into a cup shape, creating phyllo cups. Repeat the process until all cups are made.

Bake:

- Bake the phyllo cups in the preheated oven for 8-10 minutes or until they are golden brown and crispy. Keep an eye on them as they can brown quickly.

Feta and Spinach Filling:

Prepare Spinach:

- In a skillet, heat olive oil over medium heat. Add chopped spinach and sauté until wilted. Remove any excess moisture.

Mix Filling:

- In a bowl, combine the sautéed spinach, crumbled feta, ricotta cheese, grated Parmesan, minced garlic, chopped green onion, salt, black pepper, and a pinch of nutmeg if using. Mix well.

Assembly:

Fill Phyllo Cups:

- Spoon the feta and spinach filling into each baked phyllo cup, filling them to the top.

Bake Again:

- Return the filled phyllo cups to the oven and bake for an additional 10-12 minutes or until the filling is heated through and the tops are golden brown.

Serve:

- Allow the Feta and Spinach Stuffed Phyllo Cups to cool for a few minutes before serving. They can be served warm or at room temperature.

Tips:

- Be gentle when handling phyllo dough, as it can tear easily. If it dries out while you're working, cover it with a damp cloth.
- Feel free to customize the filling by adding ingredients like chopped sundried tomatoes or a sprinkle of pine nuts for extra flavor and texture.
- These stuffed phyllo cups make a great appetizer for parties or gatherings.

These Feta and Spinach Stuffed Phyllo Cups are a delightful combination of crispy phyllo pastry and a flavorful feta-spinach filling. Enjoy these bite-sized treats as an elegant appetizer!

Cajun Shrimp and Grits Bites

Ingredients:

For Grits:

- 1 cup quick-cooking grits
- 4 cups chicken or vegetable broth
- 1 cup sharp cheddar cheese, shredded
- 2 tablespoons unsalted butter
- Salt and black pepper, to taste

For Cajun Shrimp:

- 1 pound large shrimp, peeled and deveined
- 1 tablespoon Cajun seasoning
- 2 tablespoons olive oil
- 2 cloves garlic, minced
- 1 tablespoon fresh lemon juice
- Salt and black pepper, to taste
- Chopped fresh parsley, for garnish

For Assembly:

- Cherry tomatoes, halved
- Green onions, sliced

Instructions:

Grits:

Prepare Grits:
- In a medium saucepan, bring the chicken or vegetable broth to a boil. Gradually whisk in the grits, reduce heat to low, and simmer for 5-7 minutes or until the grits are cooked and thickened.

Add Cheese and Butter:
- Stir in the shredded cheddar cheese and unsalted butter until melted and well combined. Season with salt and black pepper to taste. Keep warm.

Cajun Shrimp:

Season Shrimp:
- In a bowl, toss the peeled and deveined shrimp with Cajun seasoning, minced garlic, olive oil, fresh lemon juice, salt, and black pepper. Ensure the shrimp are evenly coated.

Sauté Shrimp:
- In a skillet over medium-high heat, sauté the seasoned shrimp for 2-3 minutes on each side or until they are cooked through and have a nice Cajun crust. Remove from heat.

Assembly:

Assemble Bites:
- Spoon a small amount of cheesy grits into individual serving spoons, cups, or small bowls.

Top with Cajun Shrimp:
- Place a Cajun shrimp on top of each serving of cheesy grits.

Garnish:

- Garnish the Cajun Shrimp and Grits Bites with halved cherry tomatoes, sliced green onions, and chopped fresh parsley.

Serve:

- Serve the bites immediately, either individually or on a serving platter.

Tips:

- Adjust the level of spiciness by adding more or less Cajun seasoning to the shrimp.
- For an extra kick, you can drizzle a bit of hot sauce over the assembled Cajun Shrimp and Grits Bites.
- Customize the presentation by using small individual serving spoons or shot glasses for an elegant appetizer.

These Cajun Shrimp and Grits Bites offer a flavorful twist on a classic Southern dish. The creamy grits and spicy Cajun shrimp create a perfect combination for a tasty appetizer. Enjoy!

Brussels Sprouts Sliders with Bacon and Balsamic Glaze

Ingredients:

For Brussels Sprouts Sliders:

- 1 pound Brussels sprouts, trimmed and halved
- 2 tablespoons olive oil
- Salt and black pepper, to taste
- Slider buns or small dinner rolls

For Bacon:

- 8 slices bacon, cooked until crispy and crumbled

For Balsamic Glaze:

- 1/2 cup balsamic vinegar
- 2 tablespoons honey
- Salt, to taste

Optional Toppings:

- Goat cheese or blue cheese crumbles
- Arugula or baby spinach leaves

Instructions:

Brussels Sprouts Sliders:

   Roast Brussels Sprouts:
   - Preheat the oven to 400°F (200°C). Toss the halved Brussels sprouts with olive oil, salt, and black pepper. Roast in the oven for 20-25 minutes or until they are golden brown and crispy on the edges.

   Assemble Sliders:
   - Place a generous spoonful of the roasted Brussels sprouts on each slider bun or dinner roll.

Balsamic Glaze:

Prepare Glaze:
- In a small saucepan, combine balsamic vinegar and honey. Bring to a simmer over medium heat.

Reduce and Season:
- Reduce the heat to low and simmer for 10-15 minutes or until the mixture thickens into a glaze-like consistency. Season with a pinch of salt to taste.

Drizzle Glaze:
- Drizzle the balsamic glaze over the roasted Brussels sprouts on each slider.

Assembly:

Add Bacon:
- Sprinkle the crumbled crispy bacon over the Brussels sprouts on each slider.

Optional Toppings:
- Optionally, add a dollop of goat cheese or blue cheese crumbles on top of the bacon. Place a handful of arugula or baby spinach leaves for extra freshness.

Serve:
- Serve the Brussels Sprouts Sliders with Bacon and Balsamic Glaze immediately. Secure with toothpicks if needed.

Tips:

- You can customize the sliders by adding other toppings such as caramelized onions, avocado slices, or a drizzle of sriracha mayo.
- Choose slider buns or dinner rolls that complement the flavors, such as whole wheat or brioche buns.
- The balsamic glaze can be made in advance and stored in the refrigerator. Reheat gently before drizzling over the sliders.

These Brussels Sprouts Sliders with Bacon and Balsamic Glaze offer a delicious and unique twist on traditional sliders. The combination of roasted Brussels sprouts, crispy bacon, and sweet balsamic glaze creates a flavorful and satisfying appetizer. Enjoy!

Curry Chicken Salad on Cucumber Rounds

Ingredients:

For Curry Chicken Salad:

- 2 cups cooked chicken breast, shredded or diced
- 1/2 cup mayonnaise
- 1 tablespoon curry powder
- 1/4 cup red onion, finely chopped
- 1/4 cup celery, finely chopped
- 1/4 cup golden raisins or dried cranberries
- Salt and black pepper, to taste
- Fresh cilantro, chopped (for garnish, optional)

For Cucumber Rounds:

- 2 large English cucumbers, sliced into rounds

Instructions:

Curry Chicken Salad:

　Prepare Chicken:
- Cook chicken breasts if not already cooked. You can boil, grill, or bake them. Shred or dice the cooked chicken into bite-sized pieces.

　Make Curry Chicken Salad:
- In a bowl, combine the cooked chicken, mayonnaise, curry powder, chopped red onion, chopped celery, and golden raisins or dried cranberries. Mix until all ingredients are well combined.

　Season:
- Season the curry chicken salad with salt and black pepper to taste. Adjust the curry powder quantity based on your preference for spiciness.

Cucumber Rounds:

　Slice Cucumbers:
- Wash and slice the English cucumbers into rounds, each about 1/4 to 1/2 inch thick.

Assembly:

Top Cucumber Rounds:
- Spoon a generous portion of the curry chicken salad onto each cucumber round.

Garnish (Optional):
- Garnish the Curry Chicken Salad on Cucumber Rounds with chopped fresh cilantro if desired.

Serve:
- Arrange the assembled cucumber rounds on a serving platter and serve immediately.

Tips:

- Ensure the curry chicken salad is well-chilled before assembling on cucumber rounds for a refreshing appetizer.
- Customize the chicken salad by adding diced apples, chopped nuts (such as almonds or walnuts), or a squeeze of fresh lemon juice for additional flavor.
- Adjust the level of sweetness by varying the quantity of golden raisins or dried cranberries in the chicken salad.

These Curry Chicken Salad on Cucumber Rounds make for a light and flavorful appetizer, perfect for gatherings or as a refreshing snack. Enjoy the combination of the aromatic curry chicken with the crisp freshness of cucumber!

Blue Cheese and Walnut-Stuffed Grapes

Ingredients:

- 1 cup seedless red grapes
- 1/2 cup blue cheese, crumbled
- 1/4 cup walnuts, finely chopped
- Honey, for drizzling
- Fresh thyme leaves, for garnish (optional)
- Toothpicks or small cocktail picks

Instructions:

Prepare Grapes:
- Wash and dry the red grapes, leaving the stems intact. Make sure they are thoroughly dry to allow the cheese mixture to adhere.

Make Cheese Mixture:
- In a bowl, combine the crumbled blue cheese and finely chopped walnuts. Mix well.

Slice and Stuff Grapes:
- Using a small knife, make a small slit in each grape, creating a pocket. Be careful not to cut through the grape entirely.
- Stuff each grape with a small amount of the blue cheese and walnut mixture. Press the edges of the grape together to seal the filling inside.

Drizzle with Honey:
- Arrange the stuffed grapes on a serving platter. Drizzle honey over the stuffed grapes for a touch of sweetness.

Garnish:
- Garnish the Blue Cheese and Walnut-Stuffed Grapes with fresh thyme leaves if desired.

Secure with Toothpicks:
- If serving at a party, secure each stuffed grape with a toothpick or small cocktail pick for easy handling.

Serve:
- Serve the Blue Cheese and Walnut-Stuffed Grapes chilled or at room temperature.

Tips:

- Choose firm and ripe grapes for easier stuffing.
- Adjust the amount of blue cheese and walnuts based on your taste preferences.
- Experiment with different types of honey for varied flavors.

These Blue Cheese and Walnut-Stuffed Grapes are a delightful combination of sweet and savory, making them a perfect bite-sized appetizer for parties or gatherings. Enjoy the burst of flavors in each bite!